copyright: Copy
Al

MW01170275

This document is geared towards providing exact and reliable information with regards to the topic and issue covered. The publication is sold with the idea that the publisher is not required to render accounting, officially permitted, or otherwise, qualified services. If advice is necessary, legal or professional, a practiced individual in the profession should be ordered.

From a Declaration of Principles which was accepted and approved equally by a Committee of the American Bar Association and a Committee of Publishers and Associations.

The information herein is offered for informational purposes solely, and is universal as so. The presentation of the information is without contract or any type of guarantee assurance.
The trademarks that are used are without any consent, and the publication of the trademark is without permission or backing by the trademark owner. All trademarks and brands within this book are for clarifying purposes only and are the owned by the owners themselves, not affiliated with this document.

Disclaimer

All erudition contained in this book is given for informational and educational purposes only. The author is not in any way accountable for any results or outcomes that emanate from using this material. Constructive attempts have been made to provide information that is both accurate and effective, but the author is not bound for the accuracy or use/misuse of this information.

The Gospel of Mary Magdalene

The First Apostle Woman and Her Wisdom -
Lost Apocryphal Gospels Collection

Christopher David Richardson

Contents

Introduction

Most people today are not familiar with the Gospel of Mary. It was written in the early second century CE, but disappeared for over 1,500 years until a single, incomplete translation in Coptic surfaced in the late 1800s. We do not know how it was found, but we do know that the manuscript that contained it was bought by Carl Reinhardt in Cairo and taken to Berlin in 1896. More fragments in Greek were found in the 1900s, but a complete copy of the Gospel of Mary has not been found yet. Only about eight pages of the ancient text remain, so around half of it might be lost forever.

Despite its short length, these few pages offer an interesting look into a form of Christianity that was forgotten for a long time. This short account presents a different interpretation of Jesus' teachings as a way to gain internal spiritual knowledge. It rejects the idea that his suffering and death were the way to eternal life. It shows that the idea that Mary of Magdala was a harlot is a made-up story. It argues that women can be leaders, which is rare in early Christian writing. It criticizes corrupt authority and imagines a world where we strive for spiritual excellence. It challenges our idealized views of the unity and harmony of the first Christians. It makes us reconsider the foundation of church power. And all of this was written in the name of a woman.

The story of the Gospel of Mary is simple. As the first six pages are missing, the gospel starts in the middle of a conversation between the Savior and his disciples after his resurrection. The Savior answers their questions about the end of the physical world and sin. He teaches them that everything, whether material or spiritual, is connected. This will not be true in the end. Everything will go back to its own origin and fate. However, for now, sin is related to life in this mixed world. People sin because they do not recognize their own spiritual nature and instead value their lower nature, which misleads them and leads to illness and death. Salvation is achieved by finding the genuinely spiritual nature of humanity within oneself and overcoming physical passions and the world.

The Savior ends this lesson with a warning against those who might deceive the disciples into following a heroic leader or a set of rules. Instead, they should look inside themselves and find inner peace. After telling them to spread the gospel, the Savior leaves.

But the disciples do not go out joyfully to preach the gospel; instead, controversy erupts. All the disciples except Mary have failed to comprehend the Savior's teaching. Rather than seek peace within, they are distraught, frightened that if they follow his commission to preach the gospel, they might share his agonizing fate. Mary steps in and comforts them and, at Peter's request, relates teaching unknown to them that she had received from the Savior in a vision. The Savior had explained to her the nature of prophecy and the rise of the soul to its final rest, describing how to win the battle against the wicked, illegitimate powers that seek to keep the soul entrapped in the world and ignorant of its true spiritual nature.

But as she finishes her account, two of the disciples quite unexpectedly challenge her. Andrew objects that her teaching is strange and he refuses to believe that it came from the Savior. Peter goes further, denying that Jesus would ever have given this kind of advanced teaching to a woman, or that Jesus could possibly have preferred her to them. Apparently, when he asked her to speak, Peter had not expected such elevated teaching, and now he questions her character, implying that she has lied about having received special teaching in order to increase her stature among the disciples.

Severely taken aback, Mary begins to cry at Peter's accusation. Levi comes quickly to her defense, pointing out to Peter that he is a notorious hothead and now he is treating Mary as though she were the enemy. "We should be ashamed of ourselves," he admonishes them all; "instead of arguing among ourselves, we should go out and preach the gospel as the Savior commanded us."

The story ends here, but the controversy is far from resolved. Andrew and Peter, at least, and likely the other fearful disciples as well, have not understood the Savior's teaching and are offended by Jesus' apparent preference of a woman over them. Their limited understanding and false pride make it impossible for them to comprehend the truth of the Savior's teaching. The reader must both wonder and worry what kind of gospel such proud and ignorant disciples will preach.

How can we understand this story? It seems similar to the gospels of the New Testament, but there are also differences. The characters are familiar, like Jesus, Mary, Peter, Andrew, and Levi. They talk about the gospel and the kingdom of God, and Jesus says things like "Those who seek will find" and "Anyone with two ears should listen." In the New Testament, Jesus appears to his disciples after the resurrection, and this happens in the Gospel of Mary too. But there are also some significant differences. For example, after Jesus commissions the disciples, they don't go out to preach the gospel as they do in Matthew. Instead, they weep, afraid for their lives. Some of the things Jesus says might shock modern readers, like when he says there is no such thing as sin. Andrew thinks these teachings are strange ideas.

The Gospel of Mary was written when Christianity was new and small. There were many Christian communities spread around the Eastern Mediterranean, and they were often isolated from each other. They were small enough to meet in someone's home without attracting too much attention. At first, Christians relied on oral practices like preaching, teaching, and rituals of table fellowship and baptism. Written documents were not as important. They were only used as guides to preaching and practice. We can't assume that all the churches had the same documents. The people who wrote the first Christian literature lost most of it. Christoph Markschies thinks we have lost 85% of Christian literature from the first two centuries, and that's only the literature we know about. There must be even more because the discovery of texts like the Gospel of Mary was a surprise.

We can't reconstruct the whole of early Christian history and practice from the few surviving texts. Our picture will always be incomplete, not only because so much is lost but because early Christian practices were not tied to writing.

As a result of their distinct development and unique situations, these early churches often had divergent perspectives on key aspects of Christian doctrine and practice. Fundamental questions, such as the meaning and substance of Jesus' teachings, the nature of salvation, the authority of prophets, and the roles of women and slaves, were hotly debated. Early Christians put forth and tested competing models of the ideal community.

It is crucial to keep in mind that these first Christians did not possess a New Testament, the Nicene Creed or Apostles Creed, a universally agreed upon church hierarchy or order, church buildings, and indeed, no single view of Jesus. The elements that we might consider to be indispensable to define Christianity were nonexistent at the time. The Nicene Creed and the New Testament were the end products of these disputes and debates, rather than starting points. They symbolize the distillation of experience and experimentation, and not a negligible amount of conflict and strife.

All early Christian literature reflects these controversies. The earliest extant Christian documents, the letters of Paul, show that significant differences of opinion existed regarding issues such as circumcision, Jewish dietary laws, or the relative importance of spiritual gifts. These and other contentious topics, such as whether the resurrection was physical or spiritual, sparked theological debates and caused divisions within and between Christian communities. By the time of the Gospel of Mary, these conversations were becoming increasingly nuanced and polarized.

As we know, history is written by the victors. In the context of early Christianity, this meant that many voices in these discussions were silenced through suppression or neglect.

The Gospel of Mary, along with other recently unearthed works from the earliest days of Christianity, broadens our understanding of the tremendous variety and dynamic nature of the procedures that shaped Christianity. The objective of this volume is to enable twenty-first-century readers to hear one of those voices—not to silence the voices of canon and tradition, but to make them more audible, thanks to an expanded historical perspective. Whether or not readers choose to accept the message of the Gospel of Mary is a decision they must make for themselves.

Dialogue, Message and teachings in the Gospel

The appearances of Jesus after his resurrection are recorded in all four of the New Testament gospels and Acts, as well as in other early Christian writings such as the First Apocalypse of James and the Dialogue of the Savior. These appearances serve to confirm the reality of Jesus' resurrection, and they primarily portray the post-resurrection period as a time when Jesus imparted special teachings and commissioned his disciples to preach the gospel. The appearance of the risen Lord, the rebuke of fearful or grieving disciples, the association of special teachings with the risen Lord, the disciples as the recipients of the teachings, the mention of opponents, persecution for holding secret teachings, and a commissioning scene are all typical post-resurrection scenes.

The Savior's teachings are also heavily emphasized in the Gospel of Mary, whether in his own words or through Mary's account of the revelation to her. Although the title of the book identifies it as a "gospel," which is commonly associated with a story of Jesus' life and teachings, it meant the "good news" of the kingdom to the earliest Christians, which indicated the message and promise of the Savior rather than the genre of the work. The Gospel of Mary structured as a series of dialogues and departures, better fits the formal conventions of a post-resurrection dialogue.

These dialogues not only communicate the content of the Gospel of Mary, but they also emphasize the dialogical character of its teachings. The messages are amplified by the work's structure, which draws the reader deeper inward. The structural similarity between the two main dialogues authorizes Mary's teaching and her leadership role by placing her in a position parallel to that of the Savior. In this way, the structure of the Gospel of Mary reproduces the same message as the Savior's teaching: "Acquire my peace within yourselves... For the child of true Humanity exists within you. Follow it! Those who seek for it will find it."

Both the Savior and Mary serve as teachers in the Gospel of Mary. While the Savior answers his followers' questions, Mary shares her conversation with him. Because it requires active participation from the student, dialogue is the primary mode of instruction. The Savior's goal is to instill proper attitudes in his disciples, such as warning them not to be afraid of the dangers ahead and praising Mary for remaining calm when she saw him. By doing so, he hopes to bring his disciples up to, if not surpass, his level of understanding. After his departure, Mary is able to take his place, demonstrating the success of the Savior's teachings.

Dialogical pedagogy acknowledges the teacher's higher status but believes that this distinction is temporary and should disappear as the student progresses. To achieve freedom and efficacy, the disciples must appropriate the truth of the Savior's teachings for themselves. The Savior warns them not to rely on external authority and encourages them to look within themselves because the child of true Humanity exists within them. They can achieve a level of understanding that frees them from domination by discovering the truth for themselves.

The Possessed

And there were some females who had been cured of evil spirits and illnesses, including Mary, also known as Magdalene, who had been freed from seven demons, Joanna, the wife of Khuza (a commissioner of Herod), Susanna, and many others who supported them with their possessions.

Mary makes her first appearance in the chronology of Jesus' life in this brief passage from Luke's Gospel (8:2-3), which shows when she entered Jesus' life and why she sought him out. Jesus' reputation must have attracted her to travel the difficult ten miles from her home in Magdala to Capernaum, where he lived from 24 C.E. until the early part of 27 C.E. It's possible she came to him on foot, over rocky roads and rough paths, possessed by demons and dressed in rags. According to estimates, she sought him out in 25 C.E., after Jesus had become known in Galilee as a rabbi who welcomed sinners and fought demons that afflicted them. Although there is no evidence that Jesus visited Magdala before 25 C.E., he may have done so.

If she had started her journey from Magdala with a woolen cloak, which was desirable among travelers for shelter at night as well as coverage in rain and cold, it and any leather sandals she wore might have been stolen. However, cloaks and sandals were not affordable for every family, and the poor had to make their way barefoot, warmed only by the thick flax of their tunics. The toughness of these Galilean peasants, who spent their days outdoors even in the cold winter rains and occasional snow of the region, can only be imagined.

Luke's portrayal of Mary is not that of the wealthy and elegant temptress of medieval legend and modern fantasy. One vivid story, told and embellished in the sixth century in the Asia Minor city of Ephesus, portrays Mary as so wealthy that she was invited to a dinner with Tiberius Caesar in Rome after Jesus' death. She used the occasion to preach about Jesus' Resurrection, only to be met with imperial mockery.

The emperor stated that God would not raise the dead any more than he would change the color of the egg in Mary's hand from white to red. According to the story, the egg immediately turned red. Orthodox Christians still recount this story at Easter, and Mary and her egg are depicted in the icons of Eastern Orthodoxy.

Some contemporary scholarship has attempted to support the notion of Mary's wealth by emphasizing her association with Joanna in Luke's Gospel since Joanna had married into the prominent household of Herod Antipas, the ruler of Galilee. In one recent reconstruction, Mary and the influential Joanna were friends and business partners; Mary used Joanna's contacts and her own wealth to host dinner parties at which she employed Jesus as a comedian. Revisionist readings, like medieval legends, can stimulate and refresh our imaginations, but they also demonstrate how much the Western religious imagination desires a rich and powerful Mary to protect the poor and defenseless Jesus.

However, Luke's Gospel does not claim that Mary had the same status as Joanna; rather, it distinguishes between the two women. Joanna, who was married to a government official and was aristocratic, possibly wealthy, and well-connected, was one of the women mentioned by Luke. Mary, on the other hand, lacked Joanna's social standing and connections. Instead, she was possessed by demons. There is no evidence in ancient texts (or reasonable speculation) that Jesus ever lived in Magdala or that Mary owned property there that she gave to Jesus to use. Mary's story is not limited to her encounter with Jesus. She also plays a prominent role in the Gospel accounts of Jesus' crucifixion and resurrection. According to the Gospel of John, Mary was present at the foot of the cross with Jesus' mother and other women, while the other Gospels mention her among the women who went to the tomb on the morning of the third day after Jesus' death to anoint his body with spices.

Mary is the first person to see the risen Jesus in the Gospel of John, and he appears to her alone. This encounter marks a turning point in the Gospel, as Mary transitions from mourning the loss of her beloved teacher to proclaiming to the other disciples the good news of his resurrection. Throughout the centuries, artists, writers, and theologians have been captivated by Mary Magdalene's story. Some traditions regard her as a repentant sinner who found redemption through her encounter with Jesus, while others regard her as a saint and a model of faith and devotion. Regardless of how one interprets her story, Mary Magdalene remains an important figure in the Christian tradition and a powerful symbol of hope, transformation, and the enduring power of love.

Given Mary's demonic possession, there is little mystery about her being single. Possession carried the stigma of impurity, not the natural impurity of childbirth (for example), but the contagion of an unclean spirit. She had no doubt been ostracized in Magdala in view of her many demons. The Jews of Galilee defined themselves, in contrast to the Gentiles around them, by their devotion to stringent laws of purity that were commanded by the Torah, the Law of Moses that was written in Hebrew and passed on in oral form in the Aramaic language. What they ate, whom they could eat and associate with, how they farmed, whom they could touch or not touch, the people they could marry, the kind of sex they had and when they had it— all this and more was determined by this Torah. The Galileans' purity was their identity, more precious and delightful in their minds than prosperity under the Romans or even survival. They resorted to violent resistance sporadically during the first century to expunge the impurity the Romans had brought to their land, even when that resistance proved suicidal.

"Unclean spirits," as Jesus and his followers often called demons, inhabited Mary. These demons were considered contagious, moving from person to person and place to place, transmitted by people like Mary who were known to be possessed. In the Hellenistic world, an invisible contagion of this kind was called a daimon, the origin of the word demon. But a daimon needn't be harmful in the sources of Greco-Roman thought.

Demons hovered in the space between the terrestrial world and the realm of the gods. When Socrates was asked how he knew how to act when he faced an ethical dilemma, he said that he listened to his daimonion ti, a nameless "little daimon" that guided him.

Judaism during this period referred to the same kind of forces, using the language of spirit and distinguishing between good spirits (such as angels and the Holy Spirit that God breathed over the world) and bad spirits. Jesus called harmful spiritual influences "unclean" or "evil" spirits, and the word daimon has been used in this sense within both Judaism and Christianity. After all, even a "good" daimon from the Hellenistic world was associated with idolatry, and that is why the term demon is used in a pejorative sense in modern languages influenced by Church practices. Everyone in the ancient world, Jewish or not, agreed that demons could do harm, invading people, animals, and objects, inhabiting and possessing them. While demons are in some ways comparable to psychological complexes, they are also analogous to our bacteria, viruses, and microbes.

People protected themselves from invisible demons with the care we devote to hygiene, and ancient experts listed them the way we catalog diseases and their alleged causes. Such lists have survived on fragments of papyrus that record the ancient craft of exorcism. The fact that these experts disagreed did not undermine belief in demons any more than changing health advice today makes people skeptical of science. Then, as now, conflict among experts only heightened belief in the vital importance of the subject.

Some scholars have argued that women in early Greece were thought more susceptible of possession than men, on the dubious grounds that their vaginas made their bodies vulnerable to entry. Ancient thought was usually subtler than that, and demons do not seem to have required many apertures or much room for maneuver.

A person's eyes, ears, and nose were much more likely to expose him to their influences than any orifice below the waist. However Mary came by her demons, they rendered her unclean within the society of Jewish Galilee. She was probably very much alone when she arrived in Capernaum.

In ancient times, women who lacked family were vulnerable in ways that are difficult to fathom. The Gospels usually referred to women as sisters, wives, or mothers of men, and this connection served as their protection. As was the case in many cultures, if a married woman was alone with any man other than her husband in a private place, she could be accused of adultery (Sotah 1:1-7 Mishnah, a Rabbinic tradition that applied the Law of Moses). Similarly, a man who stayed in his future father-in-law's home could not claim later that his wife was not a virgin, as he might have had sex with her given the chance. Women without men did not make themselves available; rather, men took advantage of them.

Upon reaching puberty, a young woman transitioned from her father's custody to that of her husband. Weddings were arranged between families for mutual benefit, such as increasing their families, fields, herds, labor force, and trade connections. Marriage was a binding contract that was recorded in writing in literate communities or witnessed in illiterate peasant communities. After the marriage contract was agreed upon, a young woman stayed in her father's home for a year or so. However, even with this delay of sexual relations, pregnant fourteen- and fifteen-year-old women must have been a relatively common sight.

This arrangement was designed to preserve Israel's bloodlines' purity by managing a woman's transition from puberty to childbearing with a husband who knew he had married a virgin. Taking another man's wife was therefore punishable by death in the Torah (Leviticus 20:10). Relations with a married woman constituted the sin of adultery, while seducing a virgin could be punished more lightly (Leviticus 22:16-17), sometimes only by a fine.

Unmarried women who were no longer virgins had an unsettled, uncontrolled status that was problematic for both their families and themselves.

Men and women with Israelite mothers but whose paternity was uncertain presented a particular challenge when it came to marriage since they could not marry most other Israelites. Mary Magdalene, like Jesus, might have been a mamzer, an Israelite whose paternity was doubtful and who was therefore restricted in terms of marriage prospects.

Modern scholarship refutes the medieval tradition of portraying Mary as a prostitute at the time she met Jesus. However, encouraging one's daughter to become a prostitute was prohibited, even if she was a financial burden. The punishment for promoting or allowing prostitution is not specified (Leviticus 19:29), and prostitution did exist in and around Israel. But the practice was blamed for harming the land. The rules of purity were based on the idea that Israel had been entrusted with a land to manage carefully so that it would remain fruitful. Sinful behavior created impurity and pushed Israel toward destruction. If Israelites ceased to follow the laws of purity, God threatened that the land itself would vomit them out (Leviticus 18:3-30).

Did Mary turn to prostitution before she met Jesus? Was she raped or exploited on her journey from Magdala? These are valid questions, but no text or reasonable inference from a text answers them. To confirm or deny these possibilities takes us beyond the available evidence. However, we can say that in Mary Magdalene's time and place, as in ours, individuals who were likely victims of sin were frequently depicted as sinners themselves.

Luke's reference to Mary's seven demons contributed to the Western tradition of portraying her as a prostitute. Common paintings depict her in extravagant attire, posing in front of a mirror, or abased in shame at Jesus' feet. Medieval piety associated vanity with prostitution, arguing that women sold themselves.

But regardless of the specifics of Mary Magdalene's past, what is clear is that in her time and place, women without the protection of a male family member were vulnerable to exploitation and abuse.

Marriage was seen as the best protection for a woman, and unmarried women past a certain age were seen as troublesome and liminal figures. The rules of purity and sexual conduct were designed to protect Israel's bloodlines and ensure the continuation of a fruitful land.

Despite the lack of concrete information about Mary Magdalene's past, she has become a powerful symbol for many people. For some, she represents the possibility of redemption and transformation, as she was said to have been exorcised of seven demons by Jesus. For others, she is a feminist icon, a woman who defied the gender norms of her time by following and supporting Jesus, even after his male disciples had abandoned him.

In recent years, there has been renewed interest in Mary Magdalene and her place in the early Christian movement. Some scholars have argued that she played a more significant role in Jesus' ministry than has traditionally been recognized and that her portrayal as a reformed prostitute may have been a way for later writers to diminish her importance. Others have focused on the ways in which Mary Magdalene's story has been shaped and reshaped by different cultural and historical contexts, and how her image continues to resonate with people today.

Mary Magdalene became popular as the patron saint of flagellants by the fourteenth century, and devotion to her and to the practice of self-inflicted pain was widespread. In one story of her life, she clawed at her skin until she bled, scored her breasts with stones, and tore out her hair, all as acts of penance for her self-indulgence. She long remained the ideal icon of mortification among the lay and clerical groups that encouraged similar penances. In 1375, an Italian fraternity of flagellants carried a banner during their processions as they whipped themselves; it depicts a giant enthroned Mary Magdalene. Her head reaches into the heavens and angels surround her. At her feet kneel four white hooded figures, whose robes leave a gap at the back for ritual scourging.

Where did people in the medieval world find the material to produce such an image? Certainly not from the New Testament or from early traditions concerning Mary Magdalene. The woman whom the flagellants venerated was a combination of two different Mary: Mary Magdalene and Mary of Egypt. Mary of Egypt is herself a classic figure of Christian folklore, the whore turned ascetic. In stories that began to circulate during the sixth century, Mary of Egypt, for the sake of Christ, gave up her practice of prostitution during a pilgrimage to Jerusalem in the fourth century and lived in a cave for the rest of her life. This story was spliced into Mary Magdalene's biography.

According to this expanded tale, most famous in the thirteenth-century form in which it appears in The Golden Legend of Jacobus de Voragine, Mary traveled to France fourteen years after the Resurrection, founding churches and removing idols. In this lush legend, Mary Magdalene is confused with a completely different person in the Gospels, Mary of Bethany. This confusion provides her with a sister she never had (Martha of Bethany) as well as with a brother she never had (Lazarus). She could count on help in her missionary work from her brother Lazarus and her sister Martha, along with the aid of a boatload of Christians who had come with her and her siblings to Marseilles. Then she retreated for thirty anorexic years to an isolated cave in Provence, where she was fed miraculously during her times of prayer and meditation, when angels lifted her up to heaven.

The deep ambivalence about sexuality held by those within monastic culture did not, however, quite allow them to give up thinking about how desirable this former prostitute must have been after her conversion. She is often depicted as nude in the craggy rocks of La Sainte-Baume. Her long and lustrous hair, covering the parts of her body that modesty conventionally requires to be covered, is a staple of iconography in the West to this day, making Mary Magdalene the Lady Godiva of Christian spirituality. Mary Magdalene approached the right rabbi when she sought out Jesus.

He reveled in his reputation for consorting with allegedly loose women (the word loose being applicable to any woman who did not bear her husband's or her father's name, or some other token of male protection). There were many unattached women among Jesus' disciples; when people called him "the friend of customs-agents and sinners" (Matthew 11:19), mat wasnot a compliment, and Jesus' critics ranked these female disciples among the "sinners."

Rabbi Jesus didn't mind damning his opponents in his defense of his female followers: "Amen I say to you, that customs-agents and whores precede you into the kingdom of God!" (Matthew 21:31). That is obviously not a general endorsement of tax collection and prostitution as methods of salvation, but a tough rejoinder to people who despised his followers and called his female disciples "whores." Mary Magdalene's persistent reputation for promiscuity in medieval legend and in many modern novels rests on the mistake of presuming that women with demons were necessarily promiscuous.

Exorcism in the ancient world was not only about sex, although scholars sometimes assume that describing a person as possessed denigrates that person, even after the cure. This was not the case: Ancient thinkers knew how to distinguish a person from his or her afflictions in a way their modern counterparts might learn from. When Mary first met him, Jesus had moved from Nazareth to Capernaum after a near stoning (Luke 4:16-30) convinced him that the parochial hamlet he had known from his childhood would never accept him as a rabbi. In Capernaum, he hit his stride. This fishing town of a couple thousand people provided him with a secure haven, and his reputation as an exorcist grew.

Jesus settled in with two brothers named Simon and Andrew, who had originally come from Bethsaida (John 1:44) and had married into a fishing family in Capernaum. Following a custom in Galilee, they moved in with their in-laws, so Simon's mother-in-law was an important member of a large extended family (Mark 1:29-31).

The sturdy basalt houses of Capernaum were small and packed with people. Most were one-story dwellings, although there were occasional two-story houses, as well. Few had courtyards, and since some people kept livestock, animals joined them from time to time in their cramped homes.

Accommodating Rabbi Jesus was not a routine act of hospitality. His own needs were modest enough for a prosperous family to support, although he admitted (Luke 7:34; Matthew 11:19) that he did have a reputation of eating and drinking a great deal. The strain came more from the eager crowds that thronged around him. Venues, where Jesus practiced exorcism and healing, could become so crowded that people were unable to move. The Gospels describe a scene in a house that was so crowded that four men had to break a hole through the roof and lower their paralyzed friend to Jesus on a litter to be healed (Matthew 9:1-8; Mark 2:1-12; Luke 5:17-26). That scene suggests the environment in which Mary Magdalene first met the young rabbi. Capernaum was abuzz with Jesus' reputation— you had to fight your way in to see him.

Time and again in the Gospels, people with unclean spirits and diseases are portrayed as taking the initiative and demanding Jesus' attention, often shouting out to him and pushing through crowds to touch him. Jesus exorcised and healed by the flow of Spirit that, he said, burst forth from him and tossed out demons for the sake of God's Kingdom (Matthew 12:28; Luke 11:20). These two forces—the Spirit and God's Kingdom— were central to his practice, and they were doubtless the two energies uppermost in his mind when he treated Mary Magdalene.

God's Kingdom was a new social order that, in the mind of Jesus and his followers, was already beginning to emerge and overthrow the rule of Rome and its dominance in the territory that it came to call Provincia Syria Palaestina. Rome's rule through its local underlings seemed to break every promise God had made to Israel. The chosen people were supposed to be secure in the Promised Land; the Gentiles, Isaiah had prophesied (Isaiah 25:6-12), would make pilgrimage to Mount Zion as supplicants, not victors.

In the midst of Jewish disappointment at the advent of Roman hegemony, Jesus announced this new, divine supremacy that the Aramaic Scriptures had promised: the malkhuta delahah, "the Kingdom of God." Jesus had memorized many of these texts (which differed in significant ways from Hebrew Scripture) when he was a child, embracing the complex, rich oral tradition that was the foundation of peasant life in first-century Syria Palaestina.

Like many other rabbis of his time, Jesus could not read or write. His learning came through oral traditions, and his peculiar genius found expression in his poetry of the divine Kingdom. He gave people like Mary the inner experience of God's power, which they felt was beginning to displace the demons, impurity, poverty, and brutish Roman rule that plagued their land. Jesus taught that God's Kingdom was the revolutionary principle behind the whole cosmos: One day all of life would shimmer with divine fullness and energy. Caesar's might would dissolve, and the Kingdom would push past any resistance with a force as natural and mysterious as a sprouting seed, as inexorable as rivers in flood. People loved to hear Jesus' vision of a new age, a complete transformation of the world as they knew it. They felt themselves transformed by the many parables he wove to take them into the world where divine justice and mercy would reign supreme and transform all humanity. In his exorcisms and healings, Jesus put this vision of the transformative Kingdom into action.

The Magdalene

The name of Mary Magdalene has been associated with sensuality, penitence, and devotion for almost 2,000 years, echoing in the churches and cloisters of Vezelay in Burgundy and Saint-Maximin in Provence. Thousands of pilgrims and tourists visit Vezelay's hilltop to see the simple, welcoming, and austere Romanesque Basilica that houses the Magdalene's supposed earthly remains. The remains, a bit of bone in a glass cylinder, are framed by metallic angels and cherubim in a darkened underground chapel. During my research for this book, I also visited Vezelay, where the Romanesque crypt attracts both curious tourists and devoted worshipers.

Although a little written notice beside Mary's relics complains about the Reformation and the French Revolution disrupting her remains, it adds nothing new to her story. That complaint is a common theme of antimodernist devotion to the Magdalene in France.

Claims about the Magdalene's darker history have circulated since the thirteenth century, suggesting that she was Jesus' wife or concubine. On July 22, 1209, Crusaders dispatched by the Pope burned the town of Beziers in response to the heretical teaching that Mary and Jesus had had sexual relations. Some fifteen thousand people died that day, including the heretics and those who protected them. Recent books have linked the legend that Jesus and Mary were lovers with the myth of the Holy Grail, suggesting that the Grail was Mary's womb—the holy vessel that gave birth to Jesus' children.

The Gospels name several female followers of Jesus, who became his disciples and gathered around him in Capernaum between 24 and 27 C.E. Despite their place in Jesus' movement being beyond doubt, many churches have ignored these women, claiming that Jesus chose only twelve male disciples. However, this confusion is due, in part, to the common tendency to confuse disciples with apostles and to attribute a stature to apostles that doesn't really reflect their role in Jesus' movement.

Therefore, Mary should not be denied her standing within nascent Christianity simply because she wasn't one of the Twelve.

The fact that Mary bore the nickname "Magdalene" among Jesus' followers supports the impression that she became part of his inner circle in Capernaum. Jesus gave such names to his closest disciples, after he had known them for an extended period. But we should not assume that the nickname was a compliment, as that was not Jesus' style.

During the Renaissance, portraits of Mary Magdalene often depicted her as a stylish urban lady before her encounter with Jesus, with jewelry, a low-cut dress, and beautifully coiffed hair. Instead of portraying her as a peasant fishmonger in a stained tunic, as she likely was, these depictions added to the later legends of Mary's wealth, elegance, and seductiveness. Church dogma considered that wealth often prompted self-indulgence and indolence, sins that were not in keeping with the humble and penitent Mary who is revered today.

EXORCISM

Luke's Gospel recounts that Jesus freed Mary from "seven demons" (8:2). This number inspired hagiographers in the Middle Ages to envision Mary as struggling with all seven Deadly Sins when she first encountered Jesus. According to The Golden Legend of Jacobus de Voragine, a compendium of stories of saints compiled in the thirteenth century, Mary was extremely wealthy and owned the towns of Magdala and Bethany near Jerusalem. However, her wealth, beauty, and youth led her down a path of temptation and degradation, ultimately leading her to become a common prostitute. Medieval teachers were fearful of this path for all women.

Beyond the mediaeval preoccupation with sin and sexuality, the number seven held symbolic meaning. Seven represented completeness in ancient Hebrew, Babylonian, and Persian numerology - the eternal rhythm of creation and rest in Genesis. Israel's fascination with the number represented a version of Babylonian wisdom based on astronomical observation. In ancient Near Eastern lunar calendars, the seven-day week represented the moon's phases: four quarters waxing and waning throughout the month. This calendar was adopted by Israel, and the seven-day week is written into the structure of nature itself in Genesis (1:3-2:3).

Because seven is the symbolic number of completion and fullness, mediaeval Catholicism conceived of seven Cardinal Virtues to balance the seven Deadly Sins. Hinduism's seven chakras represent the points where spiritual energy connects with our physical bodies. In this light, Mary's "seven" demons should be viewed. The ancient mind's inherent symbolism of seven was so strong that the reference to seven demons in Luke's text does not have to be taken literally.

Mary likely underwent multiple exorcisms, which probably took about a year. Through this process, she emerged as one of Jesus' key disciples. Unlike other exorcists of his time, Jesus openly acknowledged the difficulty and danger of dealing with unclean spirits.

We don't know how many times Jesus met with Mary, and the Gospels are silent about what occurred during these sessions. Elsewhere in the New Testament (as in many other ancient pieces of literature), narrators enjoyed recounting tales of demonic possession. The possessed often shrieked, shredded their clothing, and ripped their flesh - displays that storytellers found hard to resist. However, Mary Magdalene's exorcism did not involve this type of public drama; Jesus appeared to have treated her privately.

During this lengthy healing, Jesus initiated Mary into his unique understanding of exorcism. Exorcism provides insight into Rabbi Jesus' understanding of the role of the divine Spirit in the world. He referred to demons as "unclean spirits," a term later adopted by Christian writers. People were as pure in Jesus' eyes as God created Adam and Eve. It was not solely due to contact with external objects that a person became impure or unclean. Impurity, on the other hand, was a disturbance in that person's own spirit - the "unclean spirit" - which caused them to want to be impure. Uncleanness, according to Jesus, stemmed from a disturbed desire that people had to pollute and harm themselves.

Uncleanness needed to be dealt with in the inward, spiritual personality of those afflicted. "There is nothing outside the person proceeding into one that can defile one, but what proceeds out of the person is what defiles the person" (Mark 7:15). That is why contact with people considered sinners and impure did not bother Jesus, an attitude that scandalized conventional Pharisaic teachers.

Jesus believed that God's Spirit was a more powerful force than the unclean spirits that troubled humanity. Against demonic infection, a greater force or counter contagion could prevail - the positive energy of God's purity. Defilement was an interior force of uncleanness that needed to be identified and banished by the energy of Spirit.

When Jesus taught his disciples about exorcism, he recognized the issue of serial possession, which Mary had experienced.

This teaching appears in Luke's Gospel shortly after the mention of Mary's possession (11:24-26; see also Matthew 12:43-45): "When an unclean spirit leaves a person, it travels through waterless places in search of rest, and when it finds none, it declares, 'I will return to my house from whence I came.'" It travels and discovers it swept and adorned. Then it proceeds, bringing with it seven other spirits eviler than itself, and entering dwells there. And that person's endings are worse than their beginnings."

Rabbi Jesus the exorcist speaks in this passage based on a practitioner's familiarity with demonic behavior. He knows that an unclean spirit, once out of a person, will try to find somewhere to go ("seeking repose"), and perhaps will decide to return to the person it came from ("my house"). An exorcist was not successful if a person was left in a clean-furnished house with open doors and windows waiting for a squatter. That just invited demonic repossession.

Jesus pulls back from any sweeping claim of instantly effective exorcistic power and disparages the results of quick-fix exorcisms. In contrast, the Gospels sporadically make general statements to the effect that Jesus effortlessly exorcised demons. His own words belie that claim. His reference to the demon joining up with "other spirits eviler than itself— seven!" echoes the description of Mary's possession. We cannot conclude that Jesus had Mary in mind here; after all, she was possessed by a total of seven demons in Luke's description, while Jesus spoke of seven additional demons. But her case exemplified his concern: a possession that an incautious exorcist might make repeatedly worse.

To break the cycle of possession, Jesus taught that divine Spirit had to be installed where demons had been. Mary must have been aware of how desperate she had once been, as well as the triumph her cure entailed. She required intelligence, insight, and sympathy to see Jesus' lengthy treatment through to completion. According to Rabbi Jesus' teaching, the Magdalene felt herself healed by an inner seismic shift with literally cosmic consequences because it signaled the world's transformation by the arrival of God's Kingdom.

Jesus was not always a gentle therapist. He and his followers insisted on ultimate combat with every demon because each unclean spirit represented them all. Mary became the living, breathing embodiment of the ascendance and power of Spirit. And for all the twists and turns of Christian legend, she has always stood for personal victory over evil.

Mary appears to be a mirror image of Jesus in her stark depiction of the evil she had overcome. According to the Golden Legend, Christ "embraced her in all his life," emphasizing that she became his intimate friend, constant companion, and source of help on his journeys. Petrarch referred to her as "God's sweet friend" ("dulcis arnica dei"). Here, legend develops in a way that helps us see more clearly what is already implicit in the most ancient sources: a close and lasting bond between Jesus and Mary.

But Jesus rejected these accusations and instead claimed that his power came from the Holy Spirit, which was a far greater force than any unclean spirit. He taught his disciples that exorcism was not just a matter of casting out demons, but also of replacing the void left by their departure with the positive energy of God's purity.

Jesus specifically acknowledges the problem of serial possession, which Mary had experienced, in Luke's Gospel. He teaches that once an unclean spirit has been cast out of a person, it will seek to return and may even bring other spirits with it, worsening the person's situation. To prevent repeated possession, Jesus emphasizes the importance of installing divine Spirit where demons had been.

Mary's healing involved a seismic shift in her inner being, which signaled the arrival of God's Kingdom according to Rabbi Jesus' teaching. Although Jesus was not always gentle in his approach to exorcism, he and his followers insisted on ultimate combat with each and every demon because each unclean spirit represented them all. Mary became the embodiment of the power of Spirit and an example of personal victory over evil.

Legend has developed around Mary and her relationship with Jesus, emphasizing their close and lasting bond. Jesus' opponents accused him of being in league with the powers of darkness because of his intimate relationship with Mary and his ability to cast out demons. But Jesus rejected these accusations and continued to teach his disciples about the importance of replacing the void left by the departure of unclean spirits with the positive energy of God's purity.

In its origin, the name Beelzebub has roots in the ancient pagan traditions of the Middle East. Beelzebul, the god of the underworld, was called upon in spells and sorcery during the time of Jesus to drive away demons of disease. Thus, in the context of exorcism in first-century Galilee, Jesus' Jewish opponents' accusations against him amounted to a charge of black magic.

In response, Rabbi Jesus reacted with his trademark rage and disregard for logic. He maintained that his exorcisms, like those of the Pharisees who opposed him, were beneficial. He emphasized that his exorcisms were unique in that they signaled the approaching of God's Kingdom, which would overthrow Satan's dominion. (Matthew 12:24–28)

The Pharisees accused Jesus of not being able to cast out demons except by the power of Beelzebul, ruler of the demons. Jesus retorted by questioning the logic of Satan casting out Satan, arguing that any kingdom divided against itself would be wasted. He then challenged the Pharisees by asking, "And if I by Beelzebul cast out demons, by whom do your sons cast them out?" He concluded by saying that if he cast out demons by God's Spirit, then the kingdom of God had arrived.

For Jesus and his followers, sensitivity to the world of the spirits, clean and unclean, did not disqualify Mary Magdalene as a disciple, any more than her rabbi's reputation for tackling demons with Beelzebul's authorization disqualified him as an exorcist. In fact, Jesus taught that engaging impure spirits, for all the danger involved, was what dislodged Satan from preeminence in the world, as God's Spirit ushered in God's Kingdom.

In Jesus' teachings, contact with the divine transformed unclean spirits with God's Spirit and removed their impure influence. Mary became a living symbol in Jesus' movement of the Spirit by which Jesus removed unclean spirits and brought the divine Kingdom into the human world.

A commentator in the twelfth century noted that Mary's companionship with Jesus would not have been permitted in the Church of his day. He explained that women were allowed "among the Jews" to "go about with religious men," demonstrating that he understood Judaism better than some modern interpreters. Although historical scholarship has progressed in many ways since the Middle Ages, there has been a regression in the understanding of women's and feminine roles within Judaism. Despite evidence to the contrary, modern Christians continue to propagate the false claim that women had no place in Jewish worship and learning leadership.

Mary's gender presented no obstacle to her growing influence among Jesus' disciples. In fact, being a woman was consonant with her emerging power and authority as an expert on exorcism. Rabbi Jesus conceived of the divine Spirit, the force that dissolved unclean spirits, as feminine.

Since the time of the book of Proverbs (that is, the sixth century B.C.E.), Spirit has had a secure place in Israelite theology as Yahweh's female partner. The force of Spirit that rushed out from God at the beginning of the cosmos and filled the entire universe was feminine both in the noun's gender (ruach in Hebrew) and in the life-giving creativity with which Spirit endowed creation. This divine feminine was closely associated with Wisdom, the eternal consort of Yahweh (Proverbs 8:22-31):

Yahweh possessed me at the beginning of his way, Before his works of old. From everlasting I was established, From the beginning, before the earth... When he established the heavens, I was there, When he drew a circle on the face of the deep.

When he made firm the skies above, When the fountains of the deep grew strong, When he placed the boundary of the sea, And waters did not transgress his command, When he marked the foundations of the earth, I was beside him as an architect, and I was daily his delight, Rejoicing before him always, Rejoicing in his inhabited world, And my delight was with the sons of men.

The intimacy between Wisdom and Yahweh was so deep and enjoyable that it could be described in erotic terms, and the human delight in Wisdom also promised a life of deep, rewarding pleasure. Just as God might appear by means of the three men who visited Abraham and Sarah at Mamre (Genesis 18:1-15), so divine Spirit conveyed herself with feminine traits. God's majesty was inconceivably great and varied, and it incorporated feminine as well as masculine identity.

Jesus said he spoke on behalf of Wisdom (Sophia in the Greek text of Luke) and counted himself among her envoys to the world (Luke 11:49): "Therefore also the Wisdom of God said, 'I will send them prophets and apostles, some of whom they will kill and persecute.'" Just as Jesus sent his delegates into Galilee, so he believed Wisdom had delegated him to repair a broken world. In Rabbi Jesus' mind, his whole movement amounted to an apostolic message from Spirit and therefore from Wisdom.

Western Christianity's fixation since the Middle Ages on an exclusively masculine deity tragically departs from Jesus' conception of God. Even the term for Spirit, which is feminine in Hebrew, becomes neuter in Greek and masculine in Latin, as if the process of translation itself conspired against his thought. Yet at the wellspring of his movement, male and female together reflected the reality of the divine image (Genesis 1:27), and God's Spirit conveyed the full feminine force of divinity.

We have observed that Jesus performed an exorcism on Mary Magdalene over the course of about a year, and during this time, she became more knowledgeable about his exorcism techniques than anyone else.

As a result, she became one of his primary disciples and an expert in dealing with demonic forces. Mary embodied Jesus' audacious claim in Matthew 12:28, "If I cast out demons by the power of God's Spirit, then the kingdom of God has come upon you!" This gave her a special place among his disciples because she represented the arrival of God's Kingdom. However, neither the Gospels nor scholarship recognize Mary's role as a teacher who related Jesus' exorcisms and their significance.

In other cases in the Gospels, scholars identify a source within the Gospels attributed to a prominent disciple, such as Peter, who had a similar close connection to Jesus in relation to stories or teachings. For example, Peter was the primary source of the Transfiguration story, in which he and two other apostles witnessed Jesus transformed with heavenly light and speaking with Moses and Elijah (Mark 9:2-8). Peter was the teacher within Jesus' movement who passed on this story and shaped its meaning until it was written down in the Gospels.

The Gospels do not identify their authors by name. Instead, each is simply called "According to Mark," "According to Matthew," "According to Luke," and "According to John," without any indication of who these authors were. Scholars must infer how the Gospels were produced, by whom, and in what communities of early Christians from the texts themselves.

Despite the uncertainties involved, from the start of the second century onward, thoughtful readers have recognized that the Gospels are not simply books written by individual authors working alone. Rather, they are composite editions of differing sources put together by different communities in the generations after Jesus' death. It is therefore vital to identify and analyze the Gospel sources to get at the best evidence about Jesus and to understand how the Gospels developed as literature.

One of these crucial sources was provided by Peter and his followers. They prepared people for baptism by reciting an oral narrative of what God had accomplished through Jesus.

In the Greco-Roman world, this was a complex and potentially dangerous process, as opposed to the routine baptism of infants in modern practice. During the first century, Jesus' worship was tolerated at best, and violent local pogroms occasionally erupted against the strange new Christian "superstition" (as the Romans categorized Jesus' movement). Because Christianity was perceived as a strange form of Judaism, Christians could be drawn into violent outbursts against Jews. As a result, someone claiming to want to be baptized in Jesus' name could be an informant for a city magistrate or, worse, a gang of narrow-minded thugs.

A typical year of probation was customary for converts, not only to assess their sincerity but also to ensure that they had fully learned the congregation's patterns of behavior, rituals, and prayers, refused idolatry, trusted wholeheartedly in the one God, and dedicated themselves to a life of the Spirit while resisting the material world. All these elements were integral to the Christian message, which each Gospel conveyed to its community based on earlier oral evangelism.

Peter was particularly involved in preparing converts for baptism, and passages in the Gospels that explicitly mention him or relate to his baptismal agenda likely originated from him. When scholars associate a disciple's name with their ritual agenda and the oral source they developed, they establish a kind of signature within the source. Peter is repeatedly named in passages crucial to preparing converts for baptism, indicating that he had a profound impact on shaping the Gospels.

Applying the same logic and evidence to Mary Magdalene, she emerges as the author of a source of stories that bear her oral signature. She was the most significant source of stories about Jesus' exorcisms. Because of her experience and standing, simply following Jesus put her in an ideal position to craft the detailed exorcism stories we read in the Gospels. These stories, read in order (Mark 1:21-28, 5:1-17, 9:14-29), provide a manual for dealing with unclean spirits by identifying them, confronting them with divine Spirit, and proclaiming their defeat.

They also reflect a progressive development in Jesus' ability to cope with increasingly difficult cases of possession.

The first story in the Magdalene source comes from early in Jesus' time in Capernaum, around 24 C.E. (Mark 1:21-28). The second reflects the period beginning with his flight from Herod Antipas in 27 C.E. (Mark 5:1-17), and the third appears after Jesus' Transfiguration in 30 C.E. (Mark 9:14-29). Recognizing these three exorcism stories as the core of Mary's source allows other stories to fit naturally as tributaries.

The first exorcism story, set in the Capernaum synagogue, depicts unclean spirits whose threat dissolves once they are confronted with purity (Mark 1:21-28). A close reading of the account reveals Mary Magdalene's oral signature, reflecting her insider's knowledge of the deep inner struggle involved in exorcism for a person who was possessed.

Capernaum was prosperous enough to have an actual structure for its synagogue, where the Jewish population could gather to settle local disputes, hear and discuss Scripture, delegate priestly duties, collect and transfer taxes to the Temple, and participate in rituals such as circumcision and burial. This first public act of Jesus in the Gospel According to Mark unfolds in a dignified space, a small building equipped with benches.

Mary's story describes a situation where Jesus' routine is interrupted by an unclean spirit in the synagogue. While the demon "speaks," the people in the synagogue can only hear inarticulate shrieks. However, Jesus alone understands the meaning of the sounds. The demon identifies itself with all unclean demons of the spirit world in a fascinating switch of pronouns in the text (here italicized; Mark 1:24): "We have nothing for you, Nazarene Jesus! Have you come to destroy us? I know who you are—the holy one of God!"

The slip back and forth between plural and singular has surprised many readers of Mark's text. Multiple demons—like the seven in Mary's story and the demon who found seven colleagues to repossess a person in Jesus' saying (Luke 11:24-26; Matthew 12:43-45)—signaled the resistance of the demonic world as a whole. Jesus viewed the violence of demons as part of the impending defeat of their regime, like a military commander who claims that acts by insurgents only prove they are desperate. In addition to its identification with unclean spirits as a whole, the demon in the synagogue also specifies the purpose of Jesus' exorcisms: not simple banishment, but their definitive removal from power. That is what the demon fears on behalf of the whole realm of unclean spirits: regime change instigated by Jesus as the agent of God's Kingdom, the kind of demonic retreat Mary Magdalene had experienced.

Fearing destruction, the unclean spirits act before Jesus speaks, initiating a preemptive strike by naming him. The word exorcise (ex-orkjzo in Mark's Greek) means to adjure or "to bind with an oath" (which is the aim of an exorcism). The oath was a formula that exorcists usually used to invoke divine power and force demons to obey their commands. Such spells were more effective when they identified a demon by name. In this case, however, the demon jumps in with a spell and a naming of its own. In effect, it is exorcising the exorcist, a notable departure from the well-documented form of exorcism stories in the ancient world.

Mary's source describes this as a very noisy event. The demon "cried out" (Mark 1:23). Jesus shouted back in the rough language of the street, "Shut up, and get out from him!" (v. 25). The demon's obedience came under protest; it "convulsed" its nameless victim and departed with a scream (v. 26). These acute observations all point toward a storyteller with keen knowledge of the deep combat with evil that Jesus' exorcisms involved, their raucous quality, and the danger that the exorcist would be defeated. Moreover, the storyteller knew how Jesus interpreted the demons' wordless shout (Mark 1:34), as an admission of ultimate defeat. Whoever conveyed this story had to have known both what went on and what Jesus thought about it. Mary Magdalene best fits the description of that storyteller.

By taking Mary's influence into account, we can understand why, unlike most ancient stories of exorcism, Mark's narratives depict the demons' violent resistance to Jesus instead of portraying him as a self-confident exorcist. This comes out most vividly in the second story from the Magdalene source, which is set in Decapolis, just on the other side of the Sea of Galilee from Magdala.

Several striking images, such as the possessed man's residence in a cemetery, his habit of self-harm, and his location in Gentile territory, suggest that this exorcism was aimed at addressing uncleanness as the evil that Jesus targeted in all of his exorcisms. The possessed man embodies everything unholy and is named "legion" to emphasize the source of the contagion. When Rabbi Jesus exorcised demons, he acted on behalf of the possessed, but he also acted against the source of impurity, which was Rome and Rome's collaborator, Herod Antipas.

Mary Magdalene, whose town was adjacent to Antipas's new capital, understood the reality of this uncleanness. The narrative emphasizes the struggle involved in this exorcism, as the demons were numerous, talked back to Jesus, and did not obey a direct command. The legion story deliberately engages in exaggeration, making it challenging for commentators to distinguish the story's symbolic meaning from the literal event it depicts. Nevertheless, the symbolic meaning remains clear no matter how literally we take the details: as the divine Kingdom takes root, Rome will be dislodged. Removing impurity by naming it made Satan fall, as other teachings of Jesus confirm.

Jesus became increasingly prophetic, and his words and deeds took on the character of signs, indicating how God was acting or about to act in the world. Mary Magdalene told the story of the legion of demons from the sympathetic perspective of someone who could speak from firsthand experience of being exorcised. She knew the real depth of the cosmic antagonism involved in Jesus' exorcism and had felt that antagonism in her own body.

The exorcism stories from Mary's source reflect Jesus' method of magnifying awareness that all impurity dissolves in the holiness of Spirit. In the first story, set in Capernaum's synagogue, the demon defeated itself by acknowledging the purity it confronted in Jesus, "the holy one of God," and Jesus' technique could involve giving unclean spirits what they said they wanted to speed their departure.

In the third significant story, which involves a severely possessed child, Jesus assures the anguished father that "anything is possible to one who believes" (Mark 9:23). Faith sets the stage for successful therapy, and Mary's devoted discipleship, exemplified by her journey with Jesus from Capernaum to Jerusalem, symbolizes the atmosphere of effective treatment.

Scholars have yet to scrutinize Mary's impact on the Gospels with the same intensity that they have examined Peter's, Paul's, James's, or Barnabas's. While they have had access to the relevant information in the Gospels and refined their analytic tools regarding other disciples and their sources, they have disregarded or minimized Mary's explicit connection to Jesus' exorcisms and overlooked evidence suggesting that Mary was the one who shaped and conveyed the stories of Jesus' exorcisms in the Gospels. For almost two millennia, Mary Magdalene's voice has echoed anonymously in the Gospels. It is now time to identify the speaker and appreciate her words.

Listening to Mary Magdalene's account can help us understand not only Mary herself but also a profoundly charismatic and prophetic aspect of Christianity that firmly opposes the forces of uncleanness with the power of God's Spirit.

Not all of Jesus' followers always embraced the violence of his exorcisms. We learn of this not from the Magdalene source but from other material that explains Jesus' exorcistic theory in his own words and depicts his conflict with those around him. This teaching confirms, from Jesus' perspective, precisely the sense of cosmic struggle and resistance that the Magdalene source narrates.

According to Mark's Gospel, Jesus' family once attempted to physically restrain him, perceiving him as "out of his mind" (3:21). To those who did not share Jesus' vision, he could easily appear to be mentally unstable. Rabbis during this period also described another mystic, Simon ben Zoma, as "out of his mind" because he experienced ecstasy amid everyday life.

His family's well-intentioned, conventional worry for Jesus only fueled his determination to confront Satan (Mark 3:22—27). He insisted that he was not crazy or possessed by Beelzebul. Instead, he directly battled "the strong man," the leader of all demons, in his exorcisms. Jesus stated, "No one can enter the strong man's house to plunder his goods unless he first binds the strong man; then he can plunder his house" (v. 27). Once he bound the strong man, Jesus could seize his possessions!

Jesus did not want to leave a possessed person's body open for unclean spirits to return to with even more impure companions. Instead, he would evict Satan from the house. He believed that Satan's defeat signaled the arrival of the Kingdom, and the Spirit of God, whom Jesus conceived of as female in his theology, accomplished both. When the Spirit moves in this world, she displaces demons and establishes divine justice. That is why, when discussing his exorcisms, Jesus said that denying the Holy Spirit was the only unforgivable sin (Mark 3:28-30): "Truly I tell you, people will be forgiven for their sins and whatever blasphemies they utter; but whoever blasphemes against the Holy Spirit can never have forgiveness, but is guilty of an eternal sin." The unpardonable sin is to reject the Holy Spirit as she transforms the world by vanquishing evil. The consistency of Jesus' thinking on exorcism is notable and echoes the Magdalene source.

Luke's naming of Mary in personal connection with repeated exorcisms allows us to infer that Mary Magdalene told stories about Jesus, particularly about his exorcisms, which are recounted in the Gospels today. She stands alongside the apostles who influenced how Jesus' message was preached and taught, and the exorcism stories in the Gospels bear her signature.

One of Jesus' most enduring teachings that she helped shape was about how the power from God could dissolve evil by allowing it to name itself for what it was, and she demonstrated how he put that teaching into practice. Medieval legend conveyed Mary's importance in this field in its own way. For instance, Gherardesca da Pisa, who died in 1269, described Mary as intervening in her own bloody battle with a demon and then helping her tend to her wounds.

Mary understood that the demons' most fearsome weapon, which they deployed to resist Jesus' exorcisms, was their unique knowledge of his identity. Until the first exorcism story in Mark, no one in the Gospel had referred to Jesus as "the holy one of God," a phrase that no one else would use again. By telling stories like this, Mary indicated that she knew this secret. The nameless man in the synagogue in Capernaum alone identified Jesus as "the holy one of God," while the man with the legion of demons uniquely called Jesus "Son of highest God" (Mark 5:7). As Jesus' companion in exorcism, Mary Magdalene understood that his struggle with the demons involved this messianic secret.

These inarticulate demonic cries raise a question: If the demons alone knew Jesus' spiritual identity, and he alone understood what they said, to whom did he disclose this knowledge? Once again, Mary Magdalene's oral signature leads the way to an answer. The first exorcism in Mark distinguishes Jesus as "the holy one of God," and then explains what that phrase means. The demon is an "unclean spirit," as it is elsewhere in the Gospels. As we have seen, impurity, according to Jesus' analysis, resides within a human being rather than in external objects. That which defiles originates within and spreads outward, rather than the other way around. This idea is crucial to the plot. Possession, according to Rabbi Jesus, occurred only with a person's tacit consent or inadvertence, allowing impurity to be removed through conscious intention.

43

The synagogue's unclean spirit, a source of impurity, identified Jesus as a source of purity, "the holy one of God." That is why the presence of Jesus posed a threat to that demon and the demonic world as a whole. The unspecified number of demons in the synagogue, the "legion" in the cemetery, the demon who resisted Jesus' disciples, and the "seven" who left Mary Magdalene all point to the demonic axis as a whole. Because the unclean spirits recognized purity when they experienced it, the spiritual conflict between Jesus and the forces of impurity was resolved.

Violent though their rebellion seemed, the demons ultimately recognized their own nonexistence. Their only power was denial. They could rebel against God's pure purpose, but only with the empty complaint of their own impotence. Finally, the demons had no power at all. They drowned in their own knowledge as surely as the legion did once they revealed themselves in the pigs. According to Mary's account, Rome was also headed toward the same fate.

The perspective through which the Gospels detail stories of exorcism reveals that Mary Magdalene drew from her own experiences. She had personally known the violent conflict within her own body between the demons and Jesus' desire to permanently expel them from her. The opening demonic scream, "We have nothing for you," is mirrored in the story of the man with a legion of demons. The tormented man cries out, "I have nothing for you" (Mark 5:7), and it becomes evident that "I" conceals a demonic multitude. Mary had experienced contrary and convulsive forces within her body and mind that once caused her to be at odds with herself, leading her to be controlled by impulses not her own. However, when faced with the knowledge of purity, what once seemed threatening in impurity dissolved. Obsessions ceased, and conscious choice replaced being driven by desires that were not her own. Purity within meant bodily integrity and cleanliness in action, which is the wisdom behind Jesus' exorcisms. This was wisdom that Mary had gained from her own experiences, and it made her proud to bear the nickname "the Magdalene."

Mary's role in the development of the Gospels has often been overlooked. However, it is time to acknowledge that she was a principal source in understanding Jesus' legacy. Mary's influence on how the founders of Christianity perceived the Spirit moving in the world would have been of great interest to Marguerite. The Magdalene's crucial contribution to how people in the first century understood Jesus' teachings about confronting evil in this world with the Spirit that ushers in the Kingdom of God would have assured Marguerite that someone was indeed there for her both beyond heaven's gate and in the daily struggles of life.

Jesus Teachings in the Gospel of Mary

The teachings of the Savior are at the heart of the Gospel of Mary, and Jesus is the central figure in salvation. His teachings are the key to eternal life with God, and he is referred to as the Lord and Savior. The interpretation of his teachings in the Gospel of Mary, on the other hand, differs significantly from other common understandings. While it acknowledges Jesus' death and resurrection, these events are not central to Christian belief, but rather the occasion for the disciples' mission to preach the gospel. Instead, the Gospel of Mary focuses on Jesus as a teacher and intermediary of divine revelation.

According to the Savior, after death, the human body disintegrates into the elements from which it was formed, and only the spiritual soul is immortal and lives forever. This knowledge leads people to the realization that they are spiritual beings created in the image of God, and it enables them to overcome the worldly attachments and bodily passions that lead to suffering and death. As a result, the ultimate goal of salvation is not the resurrection of the body at the end of the age, but the ascension of the soul to God, both in this life through following the Savior's teachings and at the death when the bonds between the body and the soul are loosened beyond time and eternity.

The Gospel of Mary does not teach hell or eternal punishment because God is not portrayed as a wrathful ruler or judge, but rather as the Good. Gender, sexuality, and social roles are all seen as part of the lower material realm, so God is not called Father. Even human beings' true spiritual nature is non-gendered, and they are neither male nor female, but simply Human in accordance with the divine Image of the transcendent Good. The focus of moral effort is on inner spiritual transformation rather than sin and judgement. Service to others is primarily defined as teaching people to obey the Savior's words and preaching the gospel of the Divine Realm.

The establishment of excessive laws and rules within the Christian community is seen as a tool for domination and is unnecessary for proper order.

These teachings were shaped not only in conversation and controversy with other Christians but also, as we will see, in the crucibles of ancient intellectual and social life among the diverse societies under Roman imperial rule. While Jesus and most of his earliest followers were Jews, Christianity quickly spread around the edges of the Eastern Mediterranean, from Rome to Egypt, attracting Gentile followers as well as Jews living outside of Judaea/Palestine. The earliest existing Christian literature, the letters of Paul, documents the spread of Christianity through Asia Minor to the imperial capital of Rome itself during the first decades after the death of Jesus in Jerusalem. When Gentiles encountered the teachings of Jesus, many of the earlier connections to Jewish faith and practice receded, while the belief systems and world views of the new Gentile Christians brought other issues to the fore. Tensions over whether Gentiles who accepted Jesus needed to be circumcised or follow dietary laws gave way to other concerns. Some elements already in the Jesus tradition became more prominent, especially when they intersected with philosophical speculation and popular pieties. The Gospel of Mary provides one example of these kinds of Christianity.

The Gospel of Mary presents many familiar sayings of Jesus, but they are interpreted in a framework that may seem foreign to modern readers used to reading the literature of the New Testament as part two of the Bible, following the Hebrew Scriptures of the Old Testament. Interpreting Jesus' and his followers' lives and actions as fulfilments of Hebrew Scriptures was critical to early Christian claims that faith in Christ had surpassed Judaism and that Christians were the true Israel. By the fourth and fifth centuries, this viewpoint had earned the title of orthodoxy and had condemned other points of view as heretical.

The Gospel of Mary can be viewed as an interpretation of Jesus' teachings by someone familiar with ancient philosophical piety but lacking knowledge of Judaism. It's worth noting that the prevailing perspective of orthodoxy may be so powerful and pervasive that modern readers may find the teachings "strange," as Andrew did. However, early Christians drew heavily upon popular Greek and Roman philosophy and piety, which can be seen in the canonical literature of the New Testament. Despite being written in the second century, the Gospel of Mary reflects an interpretation stream that extends far back into the early decades of first-century Christianity. Therefore, it is important to consider this work as a valuable source of insight into early Christian thought and practice.

To fully comprehend how Jesus' teachings were received among those who adhered to Platonism and Stoicism, it is necessary to provide a brief overview of some of the ideas from those traditions that most strongly intersected with the Gospel of Mary's teachings. Plato, who lived centuries before the writing of the Gospel of Mary, argued that true wisdom comes from cultivating the soul, not indulging in physical pleasures. According to Plato, death is merely the release of the soul from the body, so the wise prioritize the eternal well-being of the soul over the immediate desires of the body. Only by disciplining the body and minimizing physical contact and associations can the soul truly grasp the truth of its own nature and the truth of Reality.

When the Gospel of Mary was written, ideas from Platonists and Stoics had become pervasive in popular culture in the eastern Mediterranean. Similarly, we modern Americans are all armchair psychologists, talking about childhood traumas, neuroses, and complexes, irrespective of having read Freud. The ideas of these ancient thinkers had become removed from their original literary and intellectual contexts, and had spread over a vast geographical area, encompassing diverse cultures under the Roman empire. As a result, the social, political, and intellectual contexts within which people reflected upon such topics as human nature, justice, and ethics had shifted. In the pluralistic mix of ancient urban life, ideas that had been separate and logically incompatible began to coexist.

For instance, the Stoic ideal of apatheia could be neatly grafted onto a Platonizing, dualistic conception of ethics as conflict between the body and the immaterial soul.

Historians have a good understanding of how elite philosophers in the early Roman Empire developed Platonic and Stoic ideas. However, less is known about how these ideas were conveyed to the general population and how they were interpreted and utilized by the vast semi-literate or illiterate majority. If the Gospel of Mary is any indication of popular thought, it is evident that the teachings of Plato had evolved in ways that would have certainly surprised him. The portrait of a resurrected Jesus instructing his followers to tend to their immortal souls and eliminate their passions in the Stoic tradition so that, upon death, they can outsmart and defeat the wicked Powers who will try to impede them on their heavenly journey indicates that we have come a long way from the intellectual discussions of the male elite in Athens. By comparing the Gospel of Mary's ideas with those of Plato and the Stoics, we can to some extent determine the differences between them. There are four key similarities: the association of evil with material nature, the necessity for accurate knowledge of Reality to liberate the soul from the influence of passions, an ethical focus on conforming to the pattern of the Good, and the ascent of the soul to the Divine Realm after death.

The Body and the Word

The relationship between the body and the world has been debated by philosophers for centuries. The Gospel of Mary, an ancient Christian text, provides a unique perspective on this relationship. It is a dialogue between the Savior and his disciples. The conversation begins with a question from a disciple about the nature of the material universe. The Savior replies by saying that all material things are interconnected, have no ultimate spiritual value, and will dissolve back into their original condition, which he calls their "root."

This question and answer reflect the influence of contemporary philosophical debates about whether matter is preexistent or created. If matter is preexistent, then it is eternal, and if it is created, then it is subject to destruction. The Savior agrees that matter has no form or qualities of its own; it is simply the underlying substance that is subject to being formed or produced. He believes that everything will dissolve back into its own proper root, whether it is the result of natural causes, whether it has been molded out of formlessness, or whether it has been created from nothing. His point is clear: because the material realm is entirely destined for dissolution, it is temporary, and therefore the world and the body have no ultimate spiritual value.

Both Plato and the Gospel of Mary propose that there are two natures, one belonging to the material world and one to the Divine Realm. Evil belongs only in the material world and is associated with the finite and changing character of material reality. The nature of the Divine Realm is perfect goodness, unchanging, and eternal. The material world is the place of suffering and death, while the Divine Realm offers immortality in peace. The dualism between the material and the Divine is sharper in the Gospel of Mary than in Plato, but the Savior does not argue that the material world is evil and will be destroyed. He argues that the material world is destined to dissolve back into its original root-nature.

The idea that the world is fleeting is not new to Christian thought. Paul wrote that "the form of this world is passing away," and the Gospel of Mark says that "heaven and earth will pass away." However, the difference between these traditional Christian views and the perspective presented in the Gospel of Mary is in the understanding of what happens after the dissolution of the material world. In the traditional Christian view, the dissolution of the material world is seen as the prelude to a new creation, a new world in which righteousness dwells, and believers will live eternally with God. But in the Gospel of Mary, there is no mention of a new creation. The dissolution of the material world is understood as the final state when everything that is now mixed up together will be separated and return to its proper "root" - the material to its formless nature or nothingness, and the spiritual to its root in the Good.

This understanding of the ultimate fate of the world raises the question of how one should live in the face of the fleeting nature of the material world. The book of 2 Peter addresses this question directly, stating that "what sort of person ought you to be in lives of holiness and godliness, waiting for and hastening the coming of the day of God, because of which the heavens will be kindled and dissolved, and the elements will melt with fire!" In other words, the understanding that the material world is temporary and ultimately destined for dissolution should inspire us to live a life of holiness and godliness, as we look forward to the day when all things will be made right.

The Gospel of Mary presents a sharper dualism between the material and the Divine realm than is found in Plato. According to the Gospel, the nature of evil belongs only in the material world, and the nature of the Divine is perfect goodness, unchanging, and eternal.

Sin, Judgement and law

According to the Gospel of Mary, sin is the mixing of spiritual and material natures. The material world cannot serve as the basis for determining good and evil because attachment to it leads to sinful human conditions. Instead, one should focus on the spiritual self to attain peace of heart.

The Gospel of Mary diverges from the traditional Christian doctrine of original sin, which holds that all humans are inherently sinful due to the actions of Adam and Eve in the Garden of Eden. Instead, the text presents a more Gnostic view where the human soul is fundamentally pure and good, but trapped in a material body that is prone to deception and passion.

For the Gospel of Mary, the sin of the world is a state of ignorance and separation from one's true spiritual nature rather than a moral or legal transgression. The Savior's message focuses primarily on guiding the soul towards enlightenment and union with God, rather than emphasizing the need for repentance and forgiveness of sins. The text also stresses that matter is ultimately transient and inferior to the spiritual realm, and that the ultimate goal of the human being is to transcend the material world and return to their true spiritual nature.

In short, the Gospel of Mary provides a unique perspective on sin and the nature of human beings compared to orthodox Christian theology. The text highlights the importance of spiritual enlightenment and transcendence over moral rules and regulations and asserts that the true self is not the material body but rather the soul infused with the spirit.

The Son of Man

The phrase "Son of Man" in the Gospel of Mary is believed to mean "rrcyHpe SnpcuMe" in Coptic. This phrase represents the child of true humanity and the image of the divine realm that resides within every person. It is considered the true representation of humanity's spiritual nature and the ideal to which the disciples should aspire.

The Savior tells the disciples that "The child of true humanity exists within you" and commands them to "follow it! Those who search for it will find it". Following the child of true humanity requires identifying with the archetypal image of humanity and conforming to it as a model. This is in contrast to the interpretation of the "Son of Man" as a messianic figure in other gospel works.

The Gospel of Mary emphasizes that the true self, represented by the "Son of Man," can only be found within. The "Son of Man" in the Gospel of Mary has roots in Platonic philosophy, where the existence of a Form of Man in the divine realm apart from particular humans was posited. The gospel interprets Jesus' teachings on the child of true humanity to refer to this archetypal form of man, in connection with the creation story in Genesis 1:26-27, where humanity is created in the image of God.

In the Gospel of Mary, the Savior uses the generic term "human being" and makes both Mary and the male disciples human beings. The Gospel of Mary strives to articulate a vision of a non-gendered divine and transcendent image, with sex and gender being seen as temporary and belonging to the lower sphere of bodily existence. The divine, in this gospel, is seen as nonmaterial and nongendered, represented only by the Good, a term that can easily be grammatically neutered. Conforming to the divine image, therefore, requires abandoning distinctions, including sex and gender, and embracing the spiritual and nongendered nature of the true self.

After the Savior left, Peter asks Mary to share any words of the Savior that she knew but were unknown to the other disciples (6:1-2). Mary reports a conversation she had with the Savior. She tells the Savior that she saw a vision of him and immediately acknowledged his presence. The Savior praised her for this and said, "Blessed are you for not wavering at seeing me. For where the mind is, there is the treasure" (7:3—4). This was an important statement as "wavering" implied instability of character. Mary's stability showed her conformity to the unchanging and eternal spiritual realm, demonstrating her advanced spiritual status. The saying about treasure is often quoted in early Christian literature. In Q, a collection of Jesus' words used by the writers of Matthew and Luke, the saying is used to warn people against greed and attachment to ephemeral wealth. In the Gospel of Mary, however, the saying introduces Mary's next question and points ahead to the Savior's response. She asks whether one receives a vision by the soul or the spirit. The Savior responds that "a person does not see with the soul or with the spirit. Rather the mind, which exists between these two, sees the vision and that is what . . . " Unfortunately, the text breaks off here. However, it is clear that he is describing the tripartite composition of the true inner self, made up of soul, mind, and spirit. Enough remains of the Savior's response to offer an intriguing answer to a difficult issue: how does a prophet see a vision? The mind conveys the vision, functioning as a mediator between the spirit and the soul.

Early Christians were fully a part of ancient Mediterranean society and shared the concepts common to that culture. They believed that gods and spirits communicated with people through trances, possessions, and dreams. Christians also had differing opinions on the matter, depending on which intellectual tradition they drew upon. In the Gospel of Mary, the Savior takes a specific position on the issue. The significance of his answer to Mary can be better appreciated by comparing it with the views of the church father Tertullian, who wrote A Treatise on the Soul (De anima) at the turn of the third century. Tertullian discussed this same issue but took a different position than the Gospel of Mary.

The Gospel of Mary valued prophetic experiences highly and considered them to be authoritative for Christian teaching and practice. They believed that only the pure could see God in visions because sin and attachment to the things of the flesh dimmed the spiritual comprehension of the soul. However, they disagreed on almost every other important issue. The most fundamental basis of their disagreement rested on conflicting views about what it means to be a human being. Tertullian understood a person to be made up of a body and soul, joined in a completely unified relationship. The mind was the ruling function of the soul, not something separate from it. He maintained that the soul, as well as the body, was material. The Gospel of Mary and Tertullian also differ in their understanding of prophetic experiences. Tertullian believed that prophecy occurred through the gift of the Holy Spirit, which was given to believers at baptism. He maintained that the Holy Spirit enabled the believer to speak in tongues, interpret Scripture, and receive revelations. For Tertullian, the prophetic gift was not limited to a select few but was available to all Christians. However, he also warned against false prophets and urged Christians to test the spirits to see if they were from God (1 John 4:1). In contrast, the Gospel of Mary views prophetic experiences as the result of the soul's purification and spiritual ascent. Only the pure and holy can see God in visions, and such experiences are not available to all but are given to a select few who have attained a high level of spiritual development.

The differences between Tertullian and the Gospel of Mary reflect broader debates within early Christianity about the nature of the self, the role of prophecy, and the relationship between the material and spiritual realms. These debates were influenced by Greek philosophy, Jewish mysticism, and Christian theology, and they shaped the development of Christian doctrine and practice. The Gospel of Mary provides a glimpse into one strand of early Christian thought, which emphasized the importance of inner spiritual transformation and valued the visionary experiences of the soul. While it is a fragmentary text and much of it remains unclear, it offers a unique perspective on the spiritual aspirations and concerns of early Christians.

Controversy over the Gospel of Mary

The Gospel of Mary mainly presents the teaching of the Savior, but it also contains a significant portion of conflict among the disciples. Before the Savior left, he commanded the disciples to preach the good news, but instead of immediately setting out, they were overwhelmed with distress and doubt. Mary comforted them and turned their thoughts to the Savior's words. Her words seemed to have restored harmony among the apostles. Later, Peter addressed Mary as their "sister" and asked her to share any teachings that the Savior may have given her. Mary agreed and gave them an extensive account of a vision and dialogue she had with the Lord. However, Andrew broke in with an accusatory challenge, denying that she could have received these teachings from the Savior because they seemed strange to him. Peter was even more contentious, questioning whether the Savior would have spoken to her in private without their knowledge. Peter apparently could not accept that the Savior would have withheld such advanced teaching from the male disciples and given it to a woman.

Mary's response to Peter's request apparently went far beyond his expectations. In the Coptic version, Mary really rubs it in: she says that she has teaching that has been hidden from them. The fact that she had received a vision further emphasizes her purity of heart and mind. The Savior himself acknowledged these qualities when he said, "How wonderful you are for not wavering at seeing me." Now Mary weeps, no doubt disturbed not only because Peter is suggesting that she has made everything up and is deliberately lying to her fellow disciples, but also because of the rivalry and animosity his words suggest. At this point, Levi steps in and rebukes Peter, telling him that if he persists, he will find himself on the side of their adversaries, the Powers, rather than on the side of the Savior. Levi reminds them that they should clothe themselves with the perfect Human and go forth to preach the gospel. With the departure of Levi or all the disciples, the gospel comes to an end.

This scene raises many questions. Did the disciples accept Levi's rebuke? Did they understand Mary's teaching? Were they able to work together again, or did they go off alone, harboring resentment and misunderstanding? We don't even know who left to go preach. Some versions of the story suggest that only Levi left. What about the others? Did they just stand there? Others suggest that "they" started going out to preach. But who was included in this "they"? Mary and Levi? Andrew and Peter? All the disciples? We don't know. The Gospel of Mary is not clear about what actually happened.

The Gospel of Mary seems to side with Mary and Levi against Andrew and Peter, but it's unclear why Mary's integrity is questioned at all if the work wishes to affirm her teaching. The ending is also ambiguous. Some commentators suggest that this scene reflects real conflicts that happened in second century Christianity. Others suggest that Peter and Mary (or Peter/Andrew and Mary/Levi) represent different positions under debate or different groups in conflict with each other. However, this solution raises more questions. Does the final scene in the Gospel of Mary reflect actual conflict between the historical figures of Peter and Mary? If so, what were the tensions about? Or were Peter and Mary (Andrew and Levi) only narrative representatives for opposing Christian groups or differing theological positions? If so, who were those groups? What positions did these figures represent? And what was at stake in the conflict?

The Gospel of Mary portrays most of the disciples as fearful and uncomprehending, even antagonistic, indicating that some of them have not understood the Savior's teaching. They are still caught up in the attachment to their bodies and appear to be still under the domination of the Powers who rule the world. They have not found the child of true Humanity within or conformed to the Image of the perfect Human. The attacks of Peter and Andrew on Mary demonstrate even more convincingly that they are still under the sway of passions and false opinions; they have failed to acquire inward peace, and out of jealousy and ignorance are sowing discord among the disciples. How can they preach the gospel of the Realm of the Human One if they do not themselves understand its message?

The Gospel of Mary has put in question the practice of basing authority solely on claims of having been the Savior's disciple and having received from him a commission to preach the gospel. Even being a witness to the resurrection does not appear to have been sufficient. The Gospel of Mary does, however, portray two disciples as reliable: Mary and Levi. Both work to bring unity and harmony to the group by calling the other disciples back to consideration of the words of the Savior. Mary, in particular, is portrayed as a model disciple, comforting the other disciples and offering advanced teaching from the Savior. Both her steadfastness and her vision of the Savior demonstrate the strength of her spiritual character. It is no accident that the Savior loved her more than the others; that love and esteem are based on his sure knowledge of her. More than any other disciple, she has comprehended the Savior's teaching and is capable of teaching and preaching the gospel to others. She shows no fear at the prospect of going forth to preach because she understands how the soul overcomes the passions and advances past the Powers that attempt to dominate it. The Gospel of Mary's portrayal of Mary and Levi makes it evident that demonstrable spiritual maturity is the crucial criterion for legitimate authority. The spiritual character of the persons who preach is the ultimate and most reliable basis for judging the truth of the gospel that is preached.

This criterion fits well with ancient expectations. Teachers were supposed to manifest their teaching in their actions, providing instruction not only by what they said but by how they lived. The personal character of the teacher was considered fundamental to his or her capacity to instruct. Women teachers of philosophy were known in antiquity, although they were few in number. We have to remember too that when the Gospel of Mary was written, no rule of faith or fixed canon had yet become commonly accepted. In the early centuries, Christians often based claims for the truth of their gospel on demonstrations of the power of the Spirit in prophecy and healing or in high standards of moral living. Thus representing the steadfast and irenic character of Mary and Levi would go a long way toward establishing the Gospel of Mary's authority.

The Gospel of Mary is mainly focused on challenges to its teachings by other apostles in the Christian community. If Andrew and Peter are any indication, these challenges were mainly two-fold: 1) rejection of new teachings based on prophecy or private revelation, and 2) gender. Other Christian writings from the first and second centuries indicate that these were real issues during that time. For example, Irenaeus denied that the apostles possessed hidden mysteries delivered to them in private, and he accused heretics of inventing and preaching their own fictions. In the Gospel of Mary, Peter's accusation against Mary implies that she made up everything she was reporting. Mary's character and Levi's defense support her against these charges. Levi's defense of Mary starts by attacking Peter's character, who was known to be a hot-head, sowing division among the apostles themselves. Levi then affirms that the Savior knew Mary completely and loved her best. The Gospel of Mary emphasizes the strength of Mary's relationship with the Savior to affirm her teachings.

The Savior's judgment of Mary is illustrated by the work's portrayal of her as an unflinching and steadfast disciple, worthy of receiving visions and advanced teaching. Levi's defense is not remarkable since the standards for legitimacy are those found widely in the earliest literature: apostolic witness to the resurrection and the demonstration of spiritual gifts, in Mary's case prophetic visions and inspired teaching. All apostles in the text can claim to be witnesses to Jesus' teaching ministry, both before and after his resurrection, and all received his commission to go forth and preach the gospel. Mary's qualifications are not sufficient to defend her from attacks by fellow apostles. The crux of the defense rests on the remarkable intimacy of Mary's relationship with the Savior. As Levi states, the Savior loved Mary more than the other disciples. Andrew's objection to the "strangeness" of Mary's teaching is never explicitly answered, leaving the issue for the reader to decide. There are multiple points of contact between the revelation to Mary and the Savior's earlier teachings; however, the reader must decide whether they are sufficient to exonerate her or not.

The second challenge to Mary's authority as a teacher and apostle concerns gender, explicitly raised in the text three times. Peter acknowledges that Jesus loved Mary more than the rest of women (GMary 6:1). Peter questions Mary's credibility, asking if Jesus spoke with her in private without their knowledge, and if they are to turn around and listen to her. He also questions if Jesus chose her over them (10:3-4). Levi responds, recognizing that Peter's problem had to do with Mary being a woman, and makes it clear that the Savior did indeed love her more and gave her special teaching because she, a woman, was worthy of it.

The issue of gender is not raised merely to score a point in the interminable battle of the sexes. Mary's gender is crucial to the Gospel of Mary's theology, especially the teaching about the body and salvation. For the Gospel of Mary, bodily distinctions are irrelevant to spiritual character since the body is not the true self. Just as God is non-gendered, immaterial, and transcendent, so too is the true human self. The Savior tells his disciples that they get sick and die "because you love what deceives you" (GMary 3:7-8). Peter's fault lies in his inability to see past the distinctions of the flesh to the spiritual qualities necessary for leadership. He apparently "loves" the status his male sex-gender gives him, leading to pride and jealousy. The scene where Levi corrects Peter's ignorance helps the reader to see one of the primary ways in which people are deceived by the body.

Authority should not be based on whether one is a man or a woman, let alone on roles of socially assigned gender and sexual reproduction, but on spiritual achievement. Those who have progressed further than others have the responsibility to care and instruct them. The claim to have known Jesus and heard his words was not enough. One had to have appropriated them in one's life. Leadership is for those who have sought and found the child of true Humanity; they are to point the way for others, even as the Savior did. And such persons can be women as well as men. According to the Gospel of Mary, those who fail to understand this fact are, like Peter, mired in the materiality and passions of their lower natures.

Worse yet, they risk finding themselves on the side of the Adversaries, for those who oppose women's spiritual leadership do so out of false pride, jealousy, lack of understanding, spiritual immaturity, and contentiousness.

Rejecting the body as the self opened up the possibility of an ungendered space within the Christian community in which leadership functions were based on spiritual maturity.

The Gospel of Mary takes two strong stances regarding the basis of authority. It suggests that spiritual maturity, demonstrated through prophetic experience and unwaveringness of mind, is more reliable than mere apostolic lineage in interpreting apostolic tradition. Additionally, it suggests that spiritual maturity, rather than an individual's gender, should form the basis for leadership. On these foundations, the Gospel claims to not only possess the true understanding of Jesus' teachings, but also to have a vision of Christian community and mission that reflects the Savior's own model as a teacher and mediator of salvation.

Furthermore, the Gospel presents an alternative to the sole reliance on apostolic witness as the source of authority. Although Mary knew the historical Jesus, witnessed the resurrection, and received instruction from the Savior, these experiences are not what distinguish her from the others. Throughout the Gospel, Mary is portrayed as an exemplary disciple. She does not falter when the Savior departs, but instead steps into his place, comforting, strengthening, and instructing the others. Her spiritual comprehension and maturity are demonstrated in her calm behavior and especially in her visionary experience. These experiences provide evidence of her spiritual maturity and form the basis for her legitimate exercise of authority in instructing the other disciples. She does not teach in her own name, but instead passes on the words of the Savior, calming the disciples and turning their hearts toward the Good. Her character proves the truth of her revelation and, by extension, authorizes the teaching of the Gospel of Mary. It does so by opposing those apostles who reject women's authority and preach another gospel, laying down laws beyond those that the Savior determined.

The Gospel and acceptance into early Christianity

The Gospel of Mary was written before the canon had been established. At that time, early Christians debated the meaning of Jesus' teachings and his importance for salvation. Jesus did not write, so all portraits of him reflect the perspectives of early Christians. Historians have spent centuries investigating how those portraits developed. They have constructed the following picture: Jesus said and did some things that were remembered and passed down orally. People did not repeat everything he said and did, but only what was particularly memorable or distinctive, especially what was of use in the early churches for preaching, teaching, ritual practices, and other aspects of community life. His parables and his sayings (called aphorisms) were often so striking that they were repeated again and again. For example, a saying like "Blessed are the poor," would have surely struck people as remarkable. In the process of being passed down, his words and deeds were interpreted and elaborated.

The Gospel of Matthew interpreted the saying about poverty allegorically: "Blessed are the poor in spirit" (Matt 5:3); while the Gospel of Luke read it as a pronouncement against injustices tied to wealth and greed: "But woe to you who are rich, for you have received your consolation" (Luke 6:24). Some materials were adapted to fit the needs of developing communities for worship or mission; others were elaborated to address new situations that arose. Some sayings attributed to Jesus in the gospels came from early Christian prophets who claimed to have received revealed teaching from the Lord in the Spirit. Traditions about Jesus were used and passed down primarily in oral form as part of the living practice of early Christians. Gradually various elements of oral tradition were frozen in writing, sometimes as a collection of Jesus' words like the Gospel of Thomas, sometimes in a narrative like the Gospel of Mark.

These writings give us glimpses of how the Jesus tradition was being used and interpreted by the earliest Christians, but it would be historically incorrect to think they reflect the full breadth of early Christian interpretation of that tradition. Recent discoveries like the Gospel of Mary and the Gospel of Thomas have started to fill in some gaps, but they also prove that theological reflections in the first centuries of Christian beginnings were much more diverse and varied than we had ever realized. Moreover, only a few of the many writings by early Christians have survived. Even if all the early Christian literature had been preserved, those written sources would represent only a fraction of the full story because the gospel was spread primarily by mouth and ear: it was preached and heard. Christian ideas and practices developed in the primarily oral contexts of evangelizing, prayer and worship, preaching and prophesying.

Furthermore, the written gospels did not play the same role in early Christian life that they have in our own literate, print societies. People in ancient times were often suspicious of books. When Irenaeus argued for the authority of the four gospels in the late second century, he had to counter the views of Christians who claimed that "truth was not transmitted by means of written documents, but in living speech." True teaching was communicated directly through speech, and the most powerful and authoritative kind of speech was prophetic revelation. As the literary sources that have survived were copied and passed on, they were sometimes altered to suit new situations and theological demands. A striking example of this can be seen in the relationships among the gospels of Matthew, Mark, and Luke. The majority of scholars maintain that the authors of Luke and Matthew knew the Gospel of Mark and adapted it to fit their interpretations of Jesus' teaching and ministry. Materials could easily be added on to the end of works, like the final saying in the Gospel of Thomas (114) or the longer ending to the Gospel of Mark (16:9-20), to say nothing of both intentional and accidental changes that undoubtedly occurred in the process of manually copying the manuscripts. By the beginning of the second century, these processes had resulted in a highly diverse body of gospel material, all claiming to present the words and deeds of Jesus.

Comparison of the Gospel of Mary with other Gospel books

Paul

The Gospel of Mary has similarities with Paul's letters in terms of vocabulary and concepts. Ann Pasquier believes that Romans 7 is closely tied to Gospel of Mary 3-4.1.

GMary 3:3-8, 10-13 explains that the Savior said, "Sin doesn't exist; instead, you create sin when you act according to the nature of adultery, which is called 'sin.' For this reason, the Good came among you, pursuing what every nature deserves. It will set it within its root." Then he continued, saying, "This is why you get sick and die: because you love what deceives you. . . . Matter gave birth to a passion which has no image because it comes from what's against nature. A disturbing confusion then occurred in the whole body. That's why I told you, 'Be content at heart, but also remain discontent and disobedient; in fact, be content and agreeable only in the presence of the other image of nature.'"

GMary 4:9-10 says, "Don't make any rules beyond what I decided for you, nor create any laws like the lawgiver, or else you may be dominated by them."

Romans 7:1-8, 22-23 reads, "Do you not know, brethren—for I am speaking to those who know the law—that the law is binding on a person only during one's life? Thus a married woman is bound by law to her husband as long as he lives; but if her husband dies she is discharged from the law concerning the husband. Accordingly, she will be called an adulteress if she lives with another man when her husband is alive. But if her husband dies she is free from that law, and if she marries another man she is not an adulteress. Likewise, my brethren, you have died to the law through the body of Christ, so that you may belong to another, to him who has been raised from the dead in order that we may bear fruit for God.

While we were living in the flesh, our sinful passions, aroused by the law, were at work in our members to bear fruit for death. But now we are discharged from the law, dead to that which held us captive, so that we serve not under the old written code but in the new life of the Spirit. What then shall we say? That the law is sin? By no means! Yet if it had not been for the law, I would not have known sin. I would not have known what coveting is if the law had not said, 'You shall not covet.' But sin, finding opportunity in the commandment, wrought in me all kinds of covetousness. Apart from the law sin lies dead. ... For I delight in the law of God in my inmost self, but I see in my members another law at war with the law of my mind and making me captive to the law of sin which dwells in my members."

Pasquier lists the following points of agreement between these passages:

- The law's domination is compared to adultery.
- Adultery is compared to enslavement to passion and it leads to death.
- Freedom from the law means overcoming domination by death.
- Sin doesn't actually exist.
- Law, sin, and death are interconnected.
- An opposition is made between the divine law/nature which gives life and that fleshly law/nature which imprisons or dominates one.

According to Pasquier, the Gospel of Mary placed Paul's discussion of law into a cosmological context, transforming his attempt to understand the value of Jewish law in light of Christ's death and resurrection. This shift greatly alters the meaning of Paul's message. While Paul argues that Christ came to free humanity from sin, the Savior in the Gospel of Mary warns against adulterous attachment to the material world and the body. Unlike Paul, the Gospel of Mary does not see law as divine and purposeful (Rom 7:7, 12-14), but as a tool of domination.

It is unclear whether the author of the Gospel of Mary intentionally used this passage from Paul to change its message. There are no direct quotes, and the language and themes of passion, sin, adultery, law, and death are present in a variety of literature.

65

Since Paul's letters were being circulated widely by the second century, it is possible that readers connected the two works due to their similarities. The important issue is not whether the Gospel of Mary was influenced by Paul, but how reading the two works together would affect their meanings and theological impact.

In Romans 7-8, Paul writes to fellow Christians in Rome about how Gentiles can receive salvation through faith in Christ. His argument is centered around how they can overcome the carnal desires and passions which enslave them, and how they refuse to acknowledge the true God. Paul argues that they cannot overcome these sinful passions through the law, but only through faith in Christ's death and resurrection (or through Christ's faithfulness) can they serve God in the new life of the Spirit. The reference to adultery serves to illustrate the legal status of Gentiles before God.

In GMary 3, Jesus raises the themes of sin, adultery, and death in response to Peter's question, "What is the sin of the world?" Paul's concern for the admission of Gentiles into the community of Israel is not at issue. Instead, the problem is how to understand and overcome human enslavement to passion in view of the material nature of the body and the world. For the Gospel of Mary, sin is not a matter of right and wrong actions. Rather, it has to do with the improper mixing (adultery) of material and spiritual natures, which leads to the improper domination of the spiritual nature by the material. Salvation is achieved by overcoming attachment to the body and the material world, for it is this attachment which keeps people enslaved to suffering and death.

Both Paul and the Gospel of Mary have been misunderstood. Paul's insistence on faith as the sole route to salvation does not mean that the ethical life is not important, as the author of the Letter of James argues.

Paul and the Gospel of Mary address the issue of how to overcome sin and death. They have a similar diagnosis of the problem, that desires and passions lead to death, and a similar solution, that the life of the spirit is the key.

66

However, they differ because their views of sin and salvation are focused on different concerns and contexts. For Paul, the main issue is the relation of Gentiles to the Jewish law in the face of Christ's saving death and resurrection. In contrast, the Gospel of Mary focuses on understanding the Savior's teaching about the nature of sin and the means of overcoming suffering and death.

The actual behaviors of those who followed these two views appeared very similar, but the two groups would have understood the meaning of their behaviors quite differently. Individuals who embrace the principles presented in texts such as the Gospel of Mary or the letters of Paul have their ethical reasoning guided by the worldview and values espoused in the literature. These works not only depict reality but also present ideals of what should be. They furnish frameworks of significance that enable ethical deliberation and promote congruent conduct. Accordingly, the tales we recount and the literature we cherish play an essential role in developing our moral imagination and sentiment. The kind of narratives we are exposed to hold great importance.

The work of Paul and the Gospel of Mary provide very different orientations for thinking about what it means to be a human being. For Paul, the self is a physical, psychic, and spiritual whole. The body is thus fully part of the self, even as the soul is. Paul believed that people without faith perish at death, body and soul. There is no hint of the idea of an immortal life of punishment for unbelievers. When men die, they stay dead. Believers, on the other hand, rise to immortal life with God. The physical body is transformed into a spiritual body, immortal and freed from all mortal passions and suffering. For Paul, moral behavior is essential in purifying the body so that it can be the spiritual dwelling place of God, not in overcoming the attachment of the soul to the body, as in the Gospel of Mary.

For the Gospel of Mary, the body is not one's true self. Only the soul infused with the spirit carries the truth of what it means to be a human being. As a result, the ethical concern is focused not on catering to the desires of the body, but on strengthening the spiritual self. At death, the liberated soul is released from the body and ascends to rest with God beyond time and eternity, while the corpse returns to the inanimate material nature from which it came.

Gospel of John

In comparing the Gospel of Mary and the Gospel of John, we can see that both works focus on the role of Mary of Magdala. In John's Gospel, Jesus comforts his disciples before his departure and tells them to bear witness to the truth, even though they will face persecution. In the Gospel of Mary, Mary steps in to comfort the frightened disciples and reminds them that the Savior's grace will be with them. Both works affirm that the Savior has prepared and united his followers so that they are ready to face what he commanded them to do.

The Gospel of Mary does not assign blame to the Jews, and the disciples' fear follows the Savior's commission to go out and preach. However, Mary's message about her vision of the Savior makes it clear that not all the disciples have understood the Savior's teaching and not all are prepared to preach the gospel. Mary alone is presented as ready and able to step into the Savior's role.

While the Gospel of John affirms Mary's role as a teacher to the other disciples, their portrayals exhibit significant differences. John states that the first appearance of the resurrected Lord was to Mary, and that she was the first to use the confessional title "Lord" to refer to him. However, Mary's status is diminished in the Gospel of John in that she at first mistakes him for the gardener, and then addresses him as "Teacher" (Rabboni), indicating a relatively low standing on the hierarchical scale of Johannine Christological titles.

In the Gospel of Mary, Mary immediately recognizes the Lord when he appears and he praises her for her steadfastness of mind. She takes over many of his roles after his departure and is consistently portrayed as a model disciple and apostle. Mary's weeping is not a sign of weakness, but compassion, demonstrating her distress at both the disciples' lack of comprehension and their fomenting of discord among the apostles. In the end, Levi's speech offers a decisive defense of Mary, entirely vindicating her. The Gospel of Mary is the only text where Mary actually gets to speak in her own defense.

The Apostles

The Gospel of Mary mentions four apostles by name: Levi, Andrew, Peter, and Mary. These individuals have become legendary figures in Christianity, inspiring countless works of art and literature. Despite their immense popularity, however, we have little reliable historical information about them. The ancient evidence regarding their lives and personalities is limited. In ancient literature, the apostles are not represented as unique individuals with distinctive psychological profiles and particular biographies, but rather as types. The writers of the gospels used the apostles as malleable characters to serve their own narrative purposes. For example, in the Gospel of Mark the apostles are often portrayed as misunderstanding Jesus, which gives him the opportunity to clarify his teachings. In other works, such as the Gospel of Luke, the apostles are depicted as faithful witnesses who can attest to Jesus' teachings and deeds.

While we must acknowledge the limited historical information available, it is important to remember that these four apostles were real people who followed Jesus during his travels through Galilee and up to Jerusalem. They were all Jews, and each had a specific background: Levi was a tax collector, Andrew and Peter were brothers who worked as fishermen, and Mary was from Magdala and was the first to have a vision of the Lord. Peter also saw the risen Christ and was a key leader in the early mission.

The apostles' prestige and popularity have obscured their historical reality with myth, legend, and ritual. Nevertheless, we should strive to understand what we can about these early followers of Jesus while recognizing the limitations of the ancient evidence.

Both the gospels of Mark and Luke depict Levi as a tax collector who became a follower of Jesus (Mark 2:14; Luke 5:27-29), but neither of them mentions him in their enumeration of the twelve disciples. In the Gospel of Matthew, however, there is a narrative about a tax collector (Matt 9:9), whose name is Matthew and who is listed as one of the twelve (Matt 10:3).

This ambiguity later resulted in a tradition that sometimes identified the two, but it is not evident that Levi was commonly considered one of the twelve in the early tradition. The Gospel of John does not mention him at all. In the second-century Gospel of Philip, a certain Levi is mentioned, but he is identified only as the owner of a dye works and is unlikely to be connected to the Levi who was a tax collector (GPhil 63:26). Levi also appears in the First Apocalypse of James 37:7, but the text is so fragmentary that it is hard to draw any conclusions about his role. Therefore, it is somewhat unexpected that Levi emerges as Mary's defender in the Gospel of Mary. Could he have been selected for this task because, like Mary, he was not one of the twelve, even though he was an early disciple of Jesus? It is difficult to determine. Nonetheless, in the Gospel of Mary, he is second only to Mary in understanding the Savior's teachings. He reprimands Peter and defends Mary's character, urging the apostles to return to the Savior's instructions and to preach the gospel. In the Greek fragment, only he departs to spread the good news.

Andrew's primary claim to fame is that he was the brother of Peter, and in the earliest literature, he appears almost solely in that context. In the Gospel of Mark, he and Peter are portrayed as fishermen from Capernaum, the first of the disciples called by the Lord (Mark 1:16-18), and Andrew appears regularly in the lists of disciples in the Gospels (e.g., Mark 3:18; Matt 10:2; Luke 6:14; Acts 1:13). In the Gospel of John, he appears initially as a follower of John the Baptist, but becomes the first disciple called by Jesus and leads his brother Peter to the Lord as well (John 1:35-42). He is the only apostle mentioned by name in the surviving portion of the newly discovered Gospel of the Savior, but unfortunately, his words are lost in a gap (GSav 97:31-32).' His only other appearance in the early literature is in the Gospel of Mary, where again he appears in close conjunction with Peter and is quickly overshadowed by his brother's presence. Andrew's complaint against Mary receives no direct response either from her or from Levi, both of whom address only Peter. Andrew does not appear again in Christian literature until the end of the second century, when he becomes the hero of the Acts of Andrew, a massive work that portrays him as a miracle-working missionary sent to Achaea, northern Anatolia, Thrace, and Macedonia.

There he is active in breaking up marriages by preaching celibacy and is crucified by an enraged husband on the shore of the sea. Eventually, Andrew takes a firm place in Christian legend as the apostolic guarantor of the bishop's see of Byzantium, where his role of bringing Peter to the faith becomes a most useful tool in the polemics between Byzantium and Rome over ecclesiastical supremacy. All of this, however, occurs long after the Gospel of Mary was written, and there is no hint that the author would expect readers to associate anything with Andrew except his fraternal tie to Peter.

Historically, Peter, also known as Simon and Cephas (Mark 3:16; Matt 10:2; 16:17-19), was a fisherman from Capernaum on the Sea of Galilee (Mark 1:16-18). He accompanied Jesus throughout his ministry and was a prominent member of the inner circle of his followers. Peter was married, and it appears that his wife traveled with him on missionary journeys throughout Asia Minor (Mark 1:29-31; 1 Cor 15:5). There is some dispute about later tradition, which reports that he was martyred and buried in Rome—usually along Catholic-Protestant lines.

Peter plays a significant role in early Christian literature, and Levi's remark implying that Peter's temper and impetuosity were well-known indicates clearly that readers would be expected to know something of the tradition about him. Peter's role in the Gospel of Mary has struck some scholars as revisionary, for here Peter does not appear as the illustrious rock upon which Jesus founded the church, but rather as an ignorant hothead who sowed discord among the disciples. However, this portrait has a strong basis in early Christian tradition, a tradition that painted Peter as a complex and ambiguous character.

The Gospel of Mark, for example, recounts a scene where Jesus himself called Peter "Satan" (Mark 8:31-33): Jesus had just predicted his death and suffering, and Peter had the audacity to tell Jesus he was wrong! Once Jesus had to save Peter from drowning because his faith was too weak to walk on water (Matt 14:29-31).

At the transfiguration, his fear leads him to offer to build three booths, one each for Moses, Elijah, and Jesus (Mark 9:5-6). Still later, Peter insisted that even if everyone else abandoned Jesus, he would never do so—and this just before he denies him not once, but three times (Mark 14:29-31; 66-72), a story recounted not only in Mark, but also in the other canonical gospels. In another scene in the Gospel of John, Peter initially refuses to have Jesus wash his feet; but when Jesus says that otherwise Peter will have no part in him, Peter goes overboard in the other direction and demands that Jesus wash his hands and head as well (John 13:6-11).

In Gethsemane, when the disciples fall asleep while Jesus prays, Jesus' disappointment is directed primarily at Peter: "Simon, are you asleep? Could you not watch one hour? Watch and pray that you may not enter into temptation; the spirit indeed is willing, but the flesh is weak" (Mark 14:37-38). At the arrest, Peter pulls out a sword and cuts off the ear of the high priest's slave Malchus, earning another rebuke from Jesus (John 18:10-11). As noted earlier, even Paul had difficulties with Peter and accused him of being a hypocrite by changing his behavior to suit his audience (Gal 2:11-13). These repeated examples in the early literature consistently portray Peter as a bold fellow, but also as someone who doesn't quite understand what is going on. The Gospel of the Nazarenes took a very harsh position on Peter's character and pronounced the final judgment that Peter "denied and swore and damned himself (GNaz 19).

Peter is often characterized in a certain way, but he is also attributed to many early Christian works, such as the canonical letters of 1 and 2 Peter, the Gospel of Peter, the Letter of Peter to Philip, the Apocalypse of Peter, the Kerygma Petri, and the Acts of Peter. Although these works consistently portray Peter positively as a guarantor of apostolic authority, he remains theologically ambiguous. This is because he is used to legitimize conflicting theological positions. For example, 2 Peter claims explicit support for apostolic authority from Peter and invokes his authority against certain interpretations of Paul that the author of the letter opposed.

While Irenaeus cites Peter as a witness to the physical reality of Jesus' incarnation, the Apocalypse of Peter has him receive a revelation from the Savior that denies the incarnation and affirms that Jesus only appeared to have a body. In the Gospel of Peter, Peter appears only once in the extant fragment, but in a crucial role. The manuscript breaks off here, and what happened afterward is unknown. Still, it is highly likely that it was an account of the first resurrection appearance of Jesus.

After the second century, Peter continued to have a long and illustrious legacy in legend, art, and ecclesiastical politics as the foremost apostle of Christian faith, the co-founder of the Roman church, and the apostolic guarantor for papal authority. However, in the Gospel of Mary, Peter appears solely in his role as an ignorant hothead. His challenge to Mary presents him as a jealous man who cannot see past the weakness of the flesh to discern spiritual truth.

The earliest Christian texts, including the gospels in the New Testament, portray Mary of Magdala as a noteworthy Jewish follower of Jesus of Nazareth. Her name "Magdalene" suggests that she came from the town of Magdala (Migdal), which is located on the west coast of the Sea of Galilee (Lake Gennesaret), just north of Tiberias. Alongside other women, she went with Jesus during his ministry, was present at his crucifixion and burial, and witnessed the empty tomb. Mary of Magdala is given a significant position among Jesus' followers, particularly the women followers, in the early Christian gospel traditions. She is often listed first among the women who followed Jesus, and she is one of the main speakers in several texts from the first and second centuries that record post-resurrection dialogues between Jesus and his disciples. In the Gospel of John, the risen Jesus gives her specific instructions and commissions her to announce the good news of the resurrection to the other disciples, making her the first to proclaim the resurrection. Although Mary of Magdala is not directly referred to as an apostle, she fulfills the role, and later tradition hails her as "the apostle to the apostles." This literary tradition, attested to by multiple independent sources, suggests that Mary may have been a prophetic visionary and leader within some sector of the early Christian movement after Jesus' death.

The Gospel of Luke provides two additional details about Mary, but their historical accuracy is uncertain. Luke 8:2 identifies Mary as the one "from whom seven demons had gone out," but this is the only source to do so. Luke 8:3 mentions that Mary was financially independent and supported Jesus with her own resources, but this information may have been added at a later time when Christianity was supported by wealthy patrons. If accurate, it indicates that Mary had significant resources and was a patron of Jesus.

The Sophia of Jesus Christ, also from the second century, gives Mary a clear role as one of the seven women and twelve men gathered to hear the Savior after the resurrection, but before his ascension. Of these only five are named and speak, including Mary. At the end of his discourse, he tells them, "I have given you authority over all things as children of light," and they go forth in joy to preach the gospel. Mary is included among those special disciples to whom Jesus entrusted his most elevated teaching, and she is commissioned along with the other disciples to preach the gospel.

In the third-century text Pistis Sophia, Mary is portrayed as a prominent disciple. She asks more questions than all the rest of the disciples combined, and the Savior acknowledges that "You are she whose heart is more directed to the Kingdom of heaven than all your brothers." Mary is an active and vocal participant, with complete spiritual comprehension, who even steps in and intercedes with the Savior when the other disciples are in despair. Other narratives also portray Mary as a significant disciple.

In the Gospel of Philip, Mary Magdalene is explicitly mentioned as one of three Marys. The author wants readers to see that these figures are more than literal, historical characters. Mary is the image of a greater spiritual truth. Scholars have suggested different interpretations of this passage, based in large part on a later damaged section of the work. The Savior's intimate relationship with Mary is described, and Mary is also identified with Wisdom. The portrayal affirms the special relationship of Mary Magdalene to Jesus based on her spiritual perfection.

However, due to the limited historical information available, it is important to remember that these early followers of Jesus were real people who followed him during his travels through Galilee and up to Jerusalem. The gospels used the apostles as malleable characters to serve their own narrative purposes, and the apostles are not represented as unique individuals with distinctive psychological profiles and particular biographies, but rather as types.

Peter, who accompanied Jesus throughout his ministry and was a prominent member of the his inner circle of followers, is often characterized in a certain way, but he is also attributed to many early Christian works. Although these works consistently portray Peter positively as a guarantor of apostolic authority, he remains theologically ambiguous. This is because he is used to legitimizing conflicting theological positions.

Mary of Magdala, who is given a significant position among Jesus' followers in the early Christian gospel traditions, may have been a prophetic visionary and leader within some sectors of the early Christian movement after Jesus' death. Nevertheless, her historical accuracy is uncertain, and the information provided about her in the Gospel of Luke may have been added at a later time when Christianity was supported by wealthy patrons. For this reason, we should strive to understand what we can about these early followers of Jesus while recognizing the limitations of the ancient evidence.

Mary Magdalene is often portrayed as an exemplary disciple, but this positive symbolization of the feminine is not always consistent. It's important to note that even texts that emphasize her prominence can portray her as a controversial figure. For example, in the second-century Dialogue of the Savior, Mary is praised as "a woman who had understood completely." However, women are categorically associated with sexuality, and the works of womanhood are condemned. This hardly works to promote the status of women. Some scholars have different opinions on this passage, but Mary's response can also be read as resistance: the works of womanhood will never be obliterated.

In the Gospel of Thomas, Simon Peter wishes to exclude Mary simply because she is a woman. However, Jesus defends Mary's spiritual status by suggesting that her womanhood is not a permanent impediment to salvation. In a symbol system where "female" codes body, sexuality, and materiality, and "male" codes mind and spirit, to "become male" means that women are expected to transcend their naturally lower material natures and become spiritual beings. Jesus' statement destabilizes the categorical fixity of gender, but at best only moderates Peter's categorical sexism: women as women are not worthy of life; they need to become male.

It's important to note that while Mary Magdalene is lauded in these works, there are signs that she is becoming a center around which controversy swirls. The limited historical information available makes it challenging to draw any conclusions about Mary's role. Nonetheless, it's clear that Mary of Magdala is given a significant position among Jesus' followers, particularly the women followers, in the early Christian gospel traditions. She is often listed first among the women who followed Jesus and is one of the main speakers in several texts from the first and second centuries that record post-resurrection dialogues between Jesus and his disciples.

It's crucial to remember that these early followers of Jesus were real people who followed him during his travels through Galilee and up to Jerusalem. The gospels used the apostles as malleable characters to serve their own narrative purposes, and the apostles are not represented as unique individuals with distinctive psychological profiles and particular biographies, but rather as types. Peter, for instance, who accompanied Jesus throughout his ministry and was a prominent member of the inner circle of his followers, is often characterized in a certain way, but he is also attributed to many early Christian works. Although these works consistently portray Peter positively as a guarantor of apostolic authority, he remains theologically ambiguous. This is because he is used to legitimizing conflicting theological positions.

While there is limited historical information available, we should strive to understand what we can about these early followers of Jesus while recognizing the limitations of the ancient evidence. We should also be careful not to appropriate these works uncritically as feminist resources simply on the basis of a positive portrayal of Mary, for they can also employ feminine imagery that denigrates femaleness.

In the third-century work Pistis Sophia, Peter and Mary are shown in conflict. Mary, the most outspoken disciple in this work, wants to offer her interpretation of what has been said, but she complains that Peter threatens her and hates their race (PiSo II. 71:2). The Lord defends Mary by affirming that no power can prevent anyone filled with the Spirit of light from interpreting the things being said. However, the response is less than ideal for women. Although Mary has accused Peter of misogyny, the Savior's response does not condemn him but simply explains that anyone who is "filled with the Spirit of light," man or woman, has the capacity and the responsibility to speak. The point is that sex and gender are irrelevant to spiritual development. While the Pistis Sophia recognizes the superiority of Mary's spiritual understanding, it relegates the tasks of preaching the gospels solely to the male disciples.

The Gospel of Mary belongs to the same tradition as the figure of Mary in portraying her as a prominent disciple. However, more than any other early Christian text, it presents an unflinchingly favorable portrait of her as a woman leader among the disciples. Mary is the most prominent character and is portrayed as the ideal disciple and apostle. She is the only one who does not fear for her life at the departure of the Lord. The Savior himself praises her for her unwavering steadfastness. She is favored with a special vision of Jesus and receives advanced teaching about the fate of the soul and salvation. She comforts and instructs the other disciples, turning their attention toward the teaching of Jesus and toward the divine Good. While her teaching does not go unchallenged, in the end both the truth of her teachings and her authority to teach the male disciples are affirmed. She is portrayed as a prophetic visionary and as a leader among the disciples.

But this portrait of Mary is not the only one, as we all know. In Western European art and literature, Mary Magdalene is most often portrayed as a repentant prostitute, the Christian model of female sexuality redeemed. She stands prominently with two other figures: Eve, the temptress whose sin brought all of humanity under the judgment of death and all women into just subjugation and obedience, and Mary, the virgin mother whose impossible sexuality both idealizes and frustrates the desires of real women. Together they have formed the three-legged base upon which normative Christian models of female identity are balanced.

Where did this portrait of Mary Magdalene as a repentant whore come from? Contrary to popular Western tradition, Mary Magdalene was never a prostitute. Eastern Orthodox traditions have never portrayed her as one. She appears in the Gospel of Mary in a role closer to her actual position in early Christian history: an early and important disciple of Jesus and a leader in the early Christian movement. As with most of the other disciples, the very meagerness of what was known about Mary's life served only to fire the imaginations of later Christians, who elaborated her history in story and art according to their spiritual needs and political aims.

In contrast to the prominent role she plays in the early literature we have just discussed, the early church fathers whose writings later become the basis for orthodoxy largely ignore Mary Magdalene. When they do mention her, however, they present her in a consistently favorable light. She is usually mentioned to support points they are trying to make about the reality of the physical resurrection or the nature of the soul. Her name comes up most frequently in connection with the resurrected Jesus' enigmatic statement to her: "Do not touch me, for I have not yet ascended to the Father" (John 20:17). The fathers were concerned to counter any implication in this passage that Jesus' resurrection might not have been physical. Their concern was not unfounded, since the passage belongs to the earliest appearance narratives which were based on visionary experiences, not on encounters with a resuscitated corpse.

No criticism was directed at Mary Magdalene for Jesus' reticence about letting Mary touch him. Indeed, Tertullian praised Mary because she approached Jesus to touch him "out of love, not from curiosity, nor with Thomas' incredulity." In Tertullian's mind, the issue was simply that it was too early for touching; the resurrection had to be completed by Jesus' ascent.

From the fourth century onward, there was a clear shift in tone among the fathers, who began to have difficulty with Mary Magdalene's portrayal in the gospels. However, they confidently resolved this by creating a different understanding of her character. They argued that Mary was not worthy of touching the resurrected Lord because she lacked a full understanding of the resurrection and hence lacked true faith. She was sent to the male apostles, not to proclaim the good news of the resurrection, but rather so that her weakness could be supplemented by their strength. By conflating the account of the Gospel of John with that of the Gospel of Matthew 28:9, which tells of an appearance to at least two women, Origen confidently argued that Mary was not alone in seeing the risen Lord. The effect was to de-emphasize Mary's status as the first witness to the resurrection by making her only one member of a group. Nonetheless, the fathers confidently argued that it was appropriate for a woman to be the first to receive the redemption offered by Jesus through his resurrection, because, after all, it was a woman who had first brought sin into the world. Mary Magdalene was referred to as the second Eve, the woman whose faith in the resurrected Jesus overcame the offenses of the first Eve.

The private instruction that Mary received from the risen Jesus was a difficult problem. By the end of the second century, she had become closely associated with an interpretation of Jesus' teachings that was very different from what the church fathers were developing. The Gospel of Mary presents such teachings, and the content and the tide of the work associate these "heretical" views with Mary. Discrediting her may therefore have been in part a confident strategy of the church fathers to counter the interpretation of Jesus being spread in works like the Gospel of Mary.

It turned out that silence was not an effective strategy, since it left the imaginative field open to others. So starting in the fourth century, Christian theologians in the Latin West confidently began to construct an alternative story. The first move was to associate Mary Magdalene with the unnamed sinner who anointed Jesus' feet in Luke 7:36-50. Further confusion resulted by conflating the account in John 12:1-8, in which Mary of Bethany anoints Jesus, with the anointing by the unnamed woman in the Lukan account. From this point, identifying Mary of Magdala with Mary of Bethany was but a short step. At the end of the sixth century, Pope Gregory the Great confidently gave a sermon in which he not only identified these figures, but drew a moral conclusion that would dominate the imagination of the West for centuries to come: that Mary was the woman whom Luke calls the sinful woman, whom John calls Mary, and we believe to be the Mary from whom seven devils were ejected according to Mark. The overall picture sketched above accurately reflects the issues at stake and the positions that the church fathers took on those issues. Notably, the Eastern Churches never confused any of these Marys with unnamed prostitutes or adulteresses.

Mary Magdalene fell into the patriarchal trap of being defined primarily by her sexual roles and her relations to men, as virgins, wives, and mothers, widows, or prostitutes. As the symbolic field of the virgin and mother was already held by another Mary, and our Mary was not known to have been married or widowed, that left only the prostitute option available. It is safe to say that if Mary Magdalene had not been figured in this role, some other character would necessarily have been invented to play it. Its symbolic significance was too great to ignore.

Early on, the possibility existed that Mary Magdalene might emerge from the speculative fray as Jesus' wife and lover. The Gospel of Philip said that Jesus used to kiss her often, and in the Gospel of Mary, Peter affirmed that Jesus loved her more than other women. The third-century church father Hippolytus also used erotic imagery to allegorize the Song of Songs into an intimate relationship of the Church to Christ by treating Mary of Magdala as the Church-Bride and Jesus as the Savior-Bridegroom.

Of course, the rise of celibacy to a position of central importance in determining Christian authority structures put an official damper on these kinds of speculations. Still, the notion of an erotic relationship between Jesus and Mary Magdalene has surfaced at odd moments throughout Western history and is still capable of arousing a good deal of public ire.

Yet the role of the repentant prostitute is symbolically appealing in its own right, and not just because the other options were closed off. It has proven itself to be a much more evocative figure than that of Mary as Jesus' wife or lover. The image of Mary as the redeemed sinner has nourished a deep empathy that resonates with our human imperfection, frailty, and mortality. A fallen redeemer figure has enormous power to redeem. She holds out the possibility that purity and wholeness are never closed off; that redemption is always a possibility at hand. Despite the appropriation of sinful female sexuality for patriarchal aims, her rich tradition in story and art attests to the redemptive power of the repentant sinner.

And indeed, Mary Magdalene has been a figure of importance not just for patriarchy, where too often Gregory's praise of a woman who "immolated herself" in order to burn out "every delight she had had in herself has resulted in untold anguish, physical abuse, and self-destruction. Nonetheless, women are not only victims, but like all people are agents of their own lives, and so women have often interpreted her in ways that were unanticipated and no doubt not entirely welcomed. From the second to the twenty-first century, women prophets and preachers have continued to appeal to her to legitimate their own leadership roles.

The fact is that both women and men in Western society lack the option of an unambiguous symbolic tradition to draw upon. A confluence of historical tradition with various theological problems, patriarchal prejudices, and human affections converged to result in the complex portrait of Mary Magdalene as a repentant prostitute and preacher. The portrait was sustained over the centuries and flourished because of even more complex motives and aims.

In the end, two basic portraits of Mary Magdalene developed, each with many variations: one stressed her roles as a prominent disciple of Jesus, a visionary, and a spiritual teacher; the other painted her as a repentant prostitute whom Jesus forgave, a latter-day Eve turned from her sinful ways. While both portraits have legendary aspects, only the first has any claim to historical truth. The portrait of Mary as a repentant prostitute is pure fiction with no historical foundation whatsoever. The historical Mary of Magdala was a prominent Jewish follower of Jesus, a visionary, and a leading apostle.

The History of Christianity

So far, every analysis of the Gospel of Mary has classified it as a text belonging to the second-century heresy called Gnosticism. However, there was no religion in antiquity called Gnosticism. Scholars invented the term in the process of categorizing the variety of early Christian heresies. As we said above, they divided the earliest types into two groups: Jewish Christianity and Gnosticism. Jewish Christianity is characterized by too much or too positive an appropriation of "Judaism"; Gnosticism by too little "Judaism" or too negative an attitude toward it. Orthodoxy is just right, rejecting "Jewish error" but claiming the heritage of Scripture for its own. This typology establishes the "correct" relationship to Jewish Scripture and tradition as the single most important factor in defining normative Christian identity. These types, however, can be established only by hindsight, and even then they are not real entities, but only academic constructs. In other words, all the texts and persons grouped under these categories did exist in antiquity, but they never understood themselves to be Gnostics or Jewish Christians, let alone heretics. Calling them Gnostics is simply a shorthand method for labeling them as heretics while maintaining the appearance of impartiality. It disguises the degree to which normative interests have pervaded supposedly objective and disinterested scholarship. I never call the Gospel of Mary a Gnostic text because there was no such thing as Gnosticism.

It is true that all early Christians argued for the truth of their own theology and practice over against competing claims, but if we start out by dividing these groups into winners and losers, orthodoxy and heresy, it becomes impossible to see how early Christianity was really shaped. As I said above, this procedure obscures the complex dynamics of early Christian theology-making because it tends to treat all the "orthodox" texts primarily in terms of their similarities to each other and their differences from heresy, a procedure that obscures the real diversity of the New Testament literature and the processes by which the Nicene Creed and the canon were shaped.

So, too, the enormous theological variety of the literature classified as Gnostic gets harmonized into an overly simplified and distorting monolithic ideology. This procedure makes it appear that all Gnostic texts say more or less the same thing and permits their theology to be explained primarily in terms of how it deviates from the orthodox norm.

On the other hand, when historians set aside the anachronistic classification of early Christian literature into orthodox and heretical forms, analyzing both the similarities and the differences among the extant remains, then a much more complex picture emerges. It becomes possible to consider afresh what was at stake in how Christians formulated their beliefs and practices, and we come to see more clearly the dynamics of their interactions and the nature of the debates in which they were engaged. Eliminating these anachronistic terms of theological hindsight fosters a fundamental rethinking of the formation of early Christianity. Contemporary Christians may gain new insights and resources for reflecting on what it means to be a Christian in a pluralistic world and for addressing the pressing need to rethink the relationship of Christianity to Judaism, Islam, and other religious traditions in order to meet the demands for social well-being and justice.

We can begin by considering how the master story of Christianity has been constructed. Although Jesus and his earliest followers lived in the first century, Christianity as we know it was forged in the second to fourth centuries. These are the centuries in which creed and canon were shaped, in which the idea of the New Testament as a collection of books came into being, in which creedal statements gradually came into use as gauges of correct belief. First-century Christians had no New Testament or Nicene Creed. For most observers, this well-known fact has not seemed problematic; and since early Christians wrote and distributed these works, the New Testament texts and early creeds are indeed important primary source materials for the reconstruction of the history of early Christianity. Yet so fundamental are creed and canon to informing our very definition of what Christianity is that it is almost impossible to imagine what Christianity was like without them.

As a result, the period of Christian beginnings has almost unavoidably been read from hindsight through the lenses of later canon and creed. But if we can remove these lenses, the story of Christian beginnings may sound quite different from the way it has generally been told.

Early Christian communities were characterized by controversy over a wide range of issues. For example, the Letter to the Galatians illustrates how heated debates could become over whether Gentile men who had received salvation in Christ must undergo circumcision, and whether Christian communities should adhere to purity distinctions in their table fellowship. These issues were not battles between true Christians and heretics; instead, they represented early followers of Jesus working out what it means to be a Christian in a world where Jews and Gentiles are sharing meals together. Similarly, the differences among New Testament books are perfectly understandable once we accept that the norm of early Christianity was theological diversity, not consensus. Christian communities had access to a considerable variety of materials and produced diverse versions of Christian thought and practice, using written texts and oral traditions. Churches in different geographical areas had different written texts and oral traditions, so we cannot assume that all churches used or even knew about the same texts.

The Gospel of Mark originally ended at 16:8 with the flight of the astonished women disciples from the empty tomb. The multiformity of early Christianity becomes even more evident when we remove our canonical spectacles. All historians recognize that since the earliest churches lacked a New Testament, limiting the construction of early Christianity to the information given in the New Testament cannot give us the whole story. Historians have to take account of all those materials that are Christian, whether or not they came to reside in the canon, and even if they later were understood to be heretical. Some of the works early Christians possessed, such as the Gospel of the Hebrews or the Gospel of Barnabas, remain lost to us. Others have surfaced among the discoveries from Egypt. These new materials let us see more of the complexity and abundance of early Christian thought.

Despite the theological diversity of early Christianity, one perspective that all the New Testament texts conform to is that the death and resurrection of Jesus and his coming at the end of time are central to salvation. However, this should not lead us to believe that early Christians got their information about the content of Christian teaching and practice from written texts. Most people in the ancient Mediterranean world did not read or write. Instead, people heard about Christianity primarily through preaching and teaching and practiced Christianity through prayer, singing, and table fellowship. While the role of written texts in Christian worship or instruction is unclear, it is clear that the domination of the Bible in our own print culture is an entirely inaccurate model for imagining early Christian life.

Early Christianity was shaped by a complex set of factors, including the controversy over theological issues, diversity in Christian thought and practice, and access to a considerable variety of materials. Despite the challenges of piecing together the history of early Christianity, scholars have made great strides in recent years with the discovery of new materials that let us see more of the complexity and abundance of early Christian thought. By taking into account all those materials that are Christian, whether or not they came to reside in the canon, we can gain a more accurate understanding of the formation of early Christianity and its relevance to our modern world.

The Gospel of Thomas is a collection of sayings of Jesus, lacking any kind of storyline. It does not include accounts of Jesus' birth, death, or resurrection, but does refer to "the living Jesus" as a way of acknowledging his continuing presence. In the Gospel of Thomas, Jesus' teaching takes the focus of salvation, rather than Jesus himself: "Whoever finds the interpretation of these sayings will not experience death." Jesus cautions the disciples not to follow a leader, but to look inside themselves for the kingdom. Jesus is not portrayed as the messiah, Christ, Lord, Son of Man, or Son of God. Saying alludes to his death, but never suggests that his suffering could lead to salvation for others. Rather, Jesus is presented in terms most similar to Jewish Wisdom speculation.

In Jewish tradition, Wisdom is described as the co-creator and firstborn of God, as the light, the bringer of life and salvation, as a teacher, and as the designer and controller of history. She comes down to humanity in a variety of guises to offer her wisdom, but is rejected. Similarly, in the Gospel of Thomas, Jesus comes to humanity in the flesh, but finds everyone intoxicated with the world. His teaching gives life; it reveals what is hidden in creation yet beyond human ability to perceive. The Gospel of Thomas is meant to encourage people to seek the kingdom of God within themselves, to uncover the hidden wisdom of God in creation, and to reject worldly pursuits that lead one away from God. Above all, it is Jesus' teaching that leads people to enlightenment and salvation. The Gospel of Truth, written in the second century by theologian Valentinus, interprets Jesus, the Logos or Word of God, as the revelation of God in the world. Jesus was sent to reveal the Father, to be the presence of God in the world. He brings salvation as the teacher of divine knowledge. While the Gospel of Truth acknowledges that Jesus was persecuted and suffered on the cross, it interprets the crucifixion as the publication of his teaching. Jesus was nailed like a public notice upon a wooden pole, the cross. The Gospel of Truth interprets the wooden cross as a type of the Genesis tree of life, and Jesus as the incarnate Word, a kind of book of revelation.

The revelation of Jesus brings about a restoration to unity with the Father by eliminating the deficiencies of ignorance and destroying all the defects of suffering. It brings about authentic existence and awakens people from their nightmare-like state. The Spirit reveals the Son, and the Son's speech brings about the return to the Father, eliminating error and showing the way like a shepherd. The return to the Father does not come about through an apocalyptic catastrophe; rather, it is described as a gentle attraction, a fragrance, and merciful ointment. Souls are said to participate in the Father "by means of kisses." The work states explicitly that it is wrong to think of God as harsh or wrathful; rather, he is without evil, imperturbable, sweet, and all-knowing. The final goal of salvation is rest in the Father. Anyone who is acquainted with the New Testament gospels will find much that seems familiar in these three new gospels, for they all draw from the same pool of early Christian tradition.

Despite the considerable debate and tension among Christians during the first two centuries, early Christian theology and practice were fairly fluid affairs during this period. By the third century, lines hardened as it became increasingly clear that theological views had direct consequences for some very pressing issues. Two new texts dating from the third century, the Apocalypse of Peter and the Testimony of Truth, address some of these issues from perspectives that are new to us.

Understanding the meaning of Jesus on the cross remains an important issue for Christians. Some people agree with the views of these rediscovered texts that the figure of Jesus on the cross contradicts their belief in the goodness of God. However, for many, the image of God suffering on the cross gives meaning and redemptive power to human suffering. The issue is complex, as the symbolism of the cross has been used to justify various forms of abuse, including anti-Judaism. It has sustained suffering rather than empowering people to fight against injustice. Elisabeth Schüssler Fiorenza, a Catholic liberation theologian, argues that the redemptive power of the cross should lead people to solidarity with the poor and the suffering and give hope for resurrection. The debate over the meaning of Jesus on the cross goes to the heart of these vital issues. Examining these controversies helps to understand the meaning of Christian teachings more fully. To fully comprehend the meaning of these new materials, it is essential to read them in their own right. The later Christian tradition is so powerful that it is difficult to avoid automatically placing these new materials into the old structure of the master story. This includes assuming the normative status of the later canon and creed and reading these new materials as deviant. The perspective of the master story is ingrained not only in Christian theology but also in the imagination of historians. It is challenging to imagine that early Christians did not have a New Testament or that Jesus did not establish and authorize the religion of the Nicene Creed.

The standards of orthodoxy and heresy, the appeal to Christian origins for authorization, and the normative status of canon and creed continue to influence scholars. The new works from the Egyptian desert are proving to be very helpful.

Mary Magdalene's Works

Mary Magdalene emerged as one of Jesus' key disciples after he exorcised her. She acquired a deep understanding of Jesus' exorcism techniques and became an authority in dealing with unclean spirits. This was due to Jesus' bold claim, "If I throw out demons by God's Spirit, then the kingdom of God has arrived upon you!" However, the Gospels fail to acknowledge Mary's role as a teacher who related Jesus' exorcisms and their significance.

Scholars have identified sources within the Gospels attributed to prominent disciples like Peter. For example, Peter heads the list of the three premier apostles present at the Transfiguration, where they saw their rabbi transformed with heavenly light and speaking with Moses and Elijah (Mark 9:2-8). Evidently, Peter was the principal source of this story, the teacher within Jesus' movement who passed it on and shaped its meaning within Christianity's oral tradition until it made its way to the written Gospels.

The authors of the Gospels are not identified, with each book simply called "According to Mark," "According to Matthew," "According to Luke," and "According to John." The texts themselves infer how the Gospels were produced, by whom, and in what communities of early Christians. Despite the uncertainties involved, thoughtful readers from the start of the second century onward have recognized that the Gospels are not simply books written by individual authors working in isolation. Rather, they are composite editions of different sources that different communities put together in the generations after Jesus' death.

The Gospels emerged a generation after Jesus' death in the major centers of Christianity. Although certainty eludes any attempt to specify when and where the Gospels were composed, a consensus of scholars agrees that Mark was produced in Rome around 73 C.E.; Matthew in Damascus around 80 C.E.; Luke in Antioch on the Orontes around 90 C.E.; and John in Ephesus around 100 C.E. Identifying and analyzing the Gospel sources is vital to get at the best evidence about Jesus and to understand how the Gospels developed as literature.

Peter provided one of these crucial sources. He and his circle of followers prepared people for baptism by reciting an oral narrative of what God had accomplished with Jesus. Preparing would-be converts to Christianity involved a complex and potentially dangerous process in the Greco-Roman world, unlike the routine baptism of infants in much contemporary practice. The worship of Jesus was barely tolerated during the first century, and sometimes civic-minded enthusiasm burst out against the strange new Christian "superstition" (as the Romans categorized Jesus' movement) in the form of violent local pogroms. Because Christianity was perceived as a strange form of Judaism, Christians could also be swept up in outbursts of violence against Jews. A person who claimed to want to be baptized in Jesus' name might, in fact, be an informer for the magistrate of a city or, worse still, for a gang of narrow-minded thugs.

Peter was especially involved with preparing converts for baptism, and it makes good sense to see him as the source of passages in the Gospels that name him explicitly or that directly concern his baptismal agenda. When scholars tie together a disciple's name with the ritual agenda of that disciple and the oral source he developed, they establish what amounts to that disciple's signature within the source. In the case of Peter, he is named repeatedly within passages that were crucial to preparing converts for baptism, so it is widely agreed he had a profound influence on the formation of the Gospels.

If we apply the same logic and refer to the same kind of evidence that has been applied to Peter, Mary Magdalene also emerges as the author of a source of stories that bear her oral signature. She was the single most important conduit of stories concerning Jesus' exorcisms.

The first exorcism story, set in the Capernaum synagogue, depicts unclean spirits whose threat dissolves once they are confronted with purity. This account clearly reveals Mary Magdalene's oral signature. Her perspective governs the presentation of the story, reflecting an insider's knowledge of the deep inner struggle that exorcism involved for a person who was possessed.

Capernaum was a wealthy enough town that its Jewish population could afford to build an actual structure for its "synagogue," a designation that referred in the first century to a congregation of Israelites, with or without a building. This first public act of Jesus in the Gospel According to Mark therefore unfolds in a comparatively dignified space, a small building fitted with benches, where the assembly could comfortably settle local disputes, hear and discuss Scripture, delegate the priestly duties that local Levites fulfilled in Jerusalem, arrange for the collection and transfer of taxes to the Temple, and participate in rituals such as circumcision and burial.

In Mary's story, any routine is disrupted when an unclean spirit confronts Jesus. The demon "speaks," but the people in the synagogue hear only inarticulate shrieks. Jesus alone understands the meaning of the sounds. The demon identifies itself with all unclean demons of the spirit world in a fascinating switch of pronouns in the text "We have nothing for you, Nazarene Jesus! Have you come to destroy us? I know who you are—the holy one of God!"

Jesus viewed the violence of demons as a sign of their impending defeat. In addition to its identification with unclean spirits as a whole, the demon in the synagogue also specifies the purpose of Jesus' exorcisms: not simple banishment, but their definitive removal from power. That is what the demon fears on behalf of the whole realm of unclean spirits: regime change instigated by Jesus as the agent of God's Kingdom, the kind of demonic retreat Mary Magdalene had experienced.

Fearing destruction, the unclean spirits act before Jesus speaks, initiating a preemptive strike by naming him. Mary's source describes this as a very noisy event. The demon "cried out". Jesus shouted back in the rough language of the street, "Shut up, and get out from him!" The demon's obedience came under protest; it "convulsed" its nameless victim and departed with a scream.

These astute observations all point toward a storyteller with profound knowledge of the intense struggle with evil that Jesus' exorcisms entailed, their uproarious quality, and the peril that the exorcist would be defeated. Furthermore, the storyteller knew how Jesus interpreted the demons' wordless shout, as an admission of ultimate defeat. Whoever conveyed this story had to have known both what went on and what Jesus thought about it. Mary Magdalene best fits the description of that storyteller.

By considering Mary's influence, it becomes clear why Mark's accounts of exorcism differ from most ancient stories. Instead of portraying Jesus as a self-assured exorcist, Mark's narratives depict the demons as violently resisting him. This is particularly evident in the second story from the Magdalene source, which takes place in Decapolis, just across the Sea of Galilee from Magdala.

It was unusual in the ancient world to insist that the demons formed a violent, coordinated front of impurity, and bizarre to depict them as dictating how an exorcist should handle them. The legion story deliberately engages in exaggeration, to the point that no commentator has been able to draw the line between the story's symbolic meaning and the literal event it depicts. Still, the symbolic meaning remains clear no matter how literally we take the details: As the divine Kingdom takes root, Rome will be dislodged. Roman demons are no more threatening than panicked pigs; they will neutralize themselves in God's encompassing purity, which is as deep as the sea. Definitive exorcism signaled an ultimate change in humanity within Jesus' vision and in Mary's experience. In her narrative, the man who had been possessed with a legion of demons went on to become the first messenger of Jesus in Gentile territory. After his return from Decapolis to Galilee, Jesus sent out twelve of his disciples. They acted on his behalf, announcing the Kingdom, healing people, cleansing them of impurity, throwing out their demons. When they did so, Jesus said that he saw Satan fall like lightning from heaven, robbed of his old power. Removing impurity by naming it made Satan fall, and other teachings of Jesus unconnected with the stories Mary told confirm this perspective.

The Gospels insist on the violence of the confrontation between Jesus and unclean spirits precisely because it demonstrates the cosmic significance of his actions. As Jesus pressed home the significance of removing demons from people, he evolved as a religious persona. He became increasingly prophetic —his words and deeds took on the character of signs, indicating how God was acting or about to act in the world. Jesus and Mary Magdalene explained why demons shouted at Jesus, and he back at them: They resisted him, crying out his name and spiritual identity, because their encounter with him was a war of worlds. Mary told the story of the legion of demons from the sympathetic perspective of someone who could speak from firsthand experience of being exorcised. A legion consisted of some six thousand soldiers, and auxiliary troops co-opted by the legion could equal that number.

Although Mary's seven demons were by no means literally legion, she could tell this story because she knew the real depth of the cosmic antagonism involved in Jesus' exorcism and had felt that antagonism in her own body. Immediately before the third principal exorcism story in the Magdalene source, Jesus—transformed in divine glory and talking with Moses and Elijah—appears to Peter, James, and John. Just as he manifested himself to his disciples in the visionary experience of the Transfiguration as a master comparable to Elijah and Moses, so the story in Mary's source expresses Jesus' vehement insistence on the power of Spirit in contrast to the tentative quality of the efforts of his disciples, who had been unable to deal with the demon at hand. Jesus explained to them: "This sort can go out by nothing except by prayer."

By this time, he was heading toward his final days in Jerusalem, and Jesus had become a master exorcist, locked in cosmic struggle with Satan in a way that was beyond his followers' capacity to emulate and sometimes even to understand. As his own spirituality evolved, Jesus had found ways to magnify awareness that all impurity dissolves in the holiness of Spirit, and Mary Magdalene was there to trace that development. She knew Jesus' method in this domain inside and out, and exorcism stories from her source reflect this knowledge.

In the first story, set in Capernaum's synagogue, the demon defeated itself by acknowledging the purity it confronted in Jesus, "the holy one of God," and Jesus' technique could involve—as in the case of the "legion"—giving unclean spirits what they said they wanted to speed their departure.

Listening to Mary Magdalene's source can help us understand not only Mary, but also a charismatic and prophetic strand of Christianity rooted in Jesus' practice. This impulse, adamantly confronts the forces of uncleanness with the power of God's Spirit.

While not all of Jesus' followers embraced the violence of his exorcisms all the time, we learn of this from another run of material that spells out Jesus' exorcistic theory in his own words and represents his conflict with those around him. This teaching confirms, from Jesus' point of view, exactly the sense of cosmic struggle and resistance that the Magdalene source narrates.

Mark's Gospel indicates that once Jesus' family tried to seize him physically, thinking him to be "beside himself." If you did not share Jesus' vision, he could easily seem to be out of his mind. Rabbis of this period also characterized another mystic, Simon ben Zoma, as "beside himself" because he was prone to ecstasy in the midst of daily life.

Jesus' family's conventional concern only stoked his insistence on confrontation with Satan. He battled directly in his exorcisms with "the strong man," the honcho of all demons. Rabbi Jesus said, "No one, however, can enter the home of the strong man to rob his vessels unless he first binds the strong man, and then he will rob his home." Once he was bound, Jesus could pillage his goods! Jesus didn't want to leave a possessed person's body open for unclean spirits to return to with ever more impure companions; instead, he would sweep Satan out of house and home.

He was convinced that Satan's defeat completed the Kingdom's arrival; one implied the other, and the Spirit of God effected them both. When the Spirit—conceived of as female in Jesus' theology—moves in this world, she displaces demons and installs divine justice.

Jesus said that denying the Holy Spirit was the one sin that would not be pardoned. "Everything will be forgiven people, sins and curses (as much as they curse), but whoever curses the Holy Spirit will never ever have release but is liable for a perpetual sin." The unpardonable sin is to deny the Holy Spirit as she transforms the world by dissolving evil. The consistency of Jesus' thinking about exorcism is striking, and echoes the Magdalene source.

Luke's naming of Mary in personal connection with repeated exorcisms enables us to say that Mary Magdalene told stories about Jesus—especially the detailed stories of his exorcisms—that we can read today in the Gospels. She then takes her place beside apostles who also influenced how the message about Jesus was preached and taught. The exorcism stories in the Gospels bear her signature. One of the most vital and enduring teachings of Jesus she helped craft concerned how the power from God could dissolve evil by letting it name itself for what it was. She showed how he put that teaching into practice. Medieval legend conveyed its awareness of Mary's importance within this field in its own way. Gherardesca da Pisa, who died in 1269, spoke of Mary as intervening in her own bloody battle with a demon, then as helping her care for her wounds.

Mary knew that the demons' most fearsome weapon, deployed to resist Jesus' exorcism, was their unique knowledge of his identity. Up until the point of the first exorcism story in Mark, no one in the Gospel had called Jesus "the holy one of God." No one would ever call him that again. The demons expressed insight into Jesus' mysterious identity, what scholars for more than a century have called "the messianic secret." By telling this story and stories like it, Mary indicated that she knew this secret. The nameless man in Capernaum's synagogue alone named Jesus as "the holy one of God"; the man with the legion of demons uniquely called Jesus "Son of highest God" (Mark 5:7). Mary Magdalene, Jesus' companion in exorcism, understood the secret that his struggle with the demons involved.

The unclean spirit in the synagogue designated Jesus as a source of purity, "the holy one of God." That is why Jesus' presence was a threat to that demon and the demonic world as a whole. The unspecified number of demons in the synagogue, the "legion" in the cemetery, the demon who resisted Jesus' disciples, the "seven" who departed from Mary Magdalene—all in their different ways signal the demonic axis as a whole. The spiritual combat between Jesus and the forces of impurity was resolved because the unclean spirits recognized purity when they experienced it. Violent though their rebellion seemed, the demons ultimately recognized their own nonexistence. Their only power was denial. They could rebel against God's pure purpose, but only with the empty complaint of their own impotence. Finally, the demons had no power at all. They drowned in their own knowledge as surely as the legion did once they revealed themselves in the pigs. In Mary's telling, Rome itself headed toward the same fate.

The Gospels present only three detailed stories of the exorcisms of Jesus. In each of them, the emphasis on Jesus' assertion of the purity of Spirit, the resistance of the demonic world, impurity, struggle, and the possessed person's breakthrough to integrity come to vivid, precise expression. This oral source, which shines through the tightly coordinated but different versions in Matthew, Mark, and Luke, is the nearest approach there is to Jesus' actual technique of meeting the challenge of uncleanness and evil. Not only in cases of exorcism, which have a long history in the West, but also in Christian approaches to the miseries of addiction, compulsion, aimless violence, and purposeful wrongdoing by people and nations, the basic faith that evil named is evil removed has animated the conduct of millions of people who have read the Gospels. Mary Magdalene, anonymously but effectively, has instructed them all.

Mary Magdalene and Jesus's Movement

Mary Magdalene played a crucial role in the life and teachings of Rabbi Jesus. She emerged as the most influential woman in Jesus' movement due to her actions, teachings, and character. She was also his steadfast partner during the most difficult period of his life. This period began when Jesus was forced to flee from Capernaum under the threat of death from Herod Antipas. He spent four years wandering and experimenting with forays into Gentile territory east and west of Galilee, but his hostility to Gentile living proved incompatible with sustained residence among non-Israelites.

Mary must have traveled with Jesus during this period, witnessing his exorcisms, including the one in Decapolis. However, her travel was limited by her vulnerability as a woman, which was a significant disadvantage during that time. Jesus coordinated his movements with his other disciples, who lived in the towns and villages of Galilee, healing in the way Jesus had taught them, casting out demons, announcing the Kingdom of God, and praying and sharing meals together. Mary was part of this group, and her role extended beyond being a skilled practitioner of exorcism. She was also an adept of other spiritual practices, including anointing, which was associated with exorcism and healing.

Mary Magdalene and other women "served" or "ministered to" Jesus and his disciples, which included financial support, lodging, work with one's hands, and labor for the divine Kingdom. Mary's anointing was a form of provision at least as valuable as money. Jesus recognized that the Spirit was the engine of his action and teaching, the driving force of his exorcisms in particular. He wanted his followers to anoint people, as anointing conveyed Spirit. Mary Magdalene and her companions took up this programmatic activity, as did the more famous apostles.

The Gospel According to Luke ignores Mary Magdalene's anointing of Jesus prior to his death, which is a significant omission. Nonetheless, the story helpfully illustrates that women other than Mary Magdalene practiced anointing within Jesus' movement. Mary's anointing was a vital part of Jesus' teachings and practices, and she was its preeminent practitioner.

It is noteworthy that Jesus' teachings and practices were not limited to exorcism and anointing. He coordinated his movements with his disciples, who lived in the towns and villages of Galilee, healing in the way Jesus had taught them, casting out demons, announcing the Kingdom of God, and meditating on the presence of God's Spirit in their midst as they prayed and shared meals together. Mary was part of this group, and her role extended beyond being a skilled practitioner of exorcism. She was also an adept of other spiritual practices.

Mary Magdalene was much more than a skilled practitioner of exorcism. She was also an active participant in the pilgrimage that Jesus led to Jerusalem for the Feast of Tabernacles, where he believed he and his followers could change the world and welcome God's Kingdom into the land of Israel by offering sacrifice on Mount Zion in the way that the God of Israel desired. Following the prophecy of Zechariah, Rabbi Jesus believed that true sacrifice would bring both the end of Israel's oppression and the opening of the Temple to all humanity, both Jews and non-Jews. Mary Magdalene was with him when Jesus arrived in Jerusalem, galvanizing the festal crowds during the feast of Sukkot (or Tabernacles) in the autumn of 31 C.E. During this tumultuous period, Mary witnessed Jesus' reaction when he learned that Caiaphas, the high priest of the time, had authorized trading in the Temple, instead of maintaining the ancient practice—and Zechariah's prophecy—that Israelites offer the work of their own hands there. She observed the planning in Bethany for Jesus' onslaught on the Temple, when a small army of disciples and enthusiasts, some 150 or 200 men, joined Jesus one morning to drive out the vendors and the animals Caiaphas had allowed in the Temple's twenty-five-acre southern outer court.

She was also aware of Jesus' reaction when he discovered that one of his sympathizers in Jerusalem, a thug named Barabbas, had committed murder during the Temple raid.

MARY AT JESUS RESURRECTION AND TRANSFIGURATION

Jesus' Resurrection occurred before anyone could grasp its significance: That is the unequivocal message of Mark, the earliest Gospel, in its original form. The Gospel's climax presents a visionary experience, which Mark evokes with its spare poetry. Three women, led by Mary Magdalene, saw a vision and heard angelic words. Mark conveys their bewilderment in the face of revelation (16:1-8): And when Sabbath elapsed, Mary the Magdalene and Mary of James and Salome purchased spices so they could go anoint him. And very early on the first of the Sabbaths they came upon the tomb when the sun dawned. And they were saying to one another, Who will roll the stone away from the opening of the tomb for us? They looked up and perceived that the stone had been rolled off (because it was exceedingly big). They went towards the tomb and saw a young man sitting on the right appareled in a white robe, and they were completely astonished.

But he says to them: "Do not be completely astonished. You see't Jesus the crucified Nazarene. He is raised; he is not here. Look—the place where they laid him. But depart, tell his students and Peter that he goes before you into Galilee; you will see him there, just as he said to you". They went out and fled from the tomb, because trembling and frenzy had them. And they said nothing to any one; they were afraid, because— This abrupt ending climaxes the primitive but effective art of Mark, signaling how hard and disruptive it was, even for those intimate with Jesus, to grapple with the vision that signaled he had overcome death. From a prosaic point of view, this truncated finale makes the Gospel seem defective. How could anyone end a story by saying "they were afraid, because—"? In later manuscripts of Mark, this apparent gap was dutifully filled in with now-familiar stories culled from the other Gospels of the risen Jesus appearing to his disciples. Pious scribes frequently harmonized the texts of the Gospels, making them look alike. These additions are transparent, and Mark's stark, primitive ending, the apogee of its art of revelation, stands out because of its powerful originality.

In the Gospel's original form, the three women are the first to know that Jesus had been raised from the dead. Mark names Mary Magdalene first in this account and her cognomen, "the Magdalene," resonates, as I mentioned in chapter 2, with Jesus"—"the Nazarene." Mary is on her way with Mary of James and Salome to anoint Jesus' corpse, and that reinforces the point made in chapter 5—that the Magdalene had been the nameless anointer who prepared Jesus before his death for burial. Mary's every action and response are crucial to an understanding of her realization that God had raised Jesus from the dead. It was customary, as well as a commandment of the Torah, that Israelites attend to the corpses of relatives and friends, even victims of crucifixion. A first-century ossuary, discovered outside Jerusalem in 1968, contains the bones of a young man named Yochanan. An iron spike with an attached piece of wood is embedded in his right heel. Properly tending to the dead was incumbent on every Israelite, and any Roman official would court rebellion by deliberately flouting that imperative. The Jerusalem prefect must have released Yochanan's broken body for burial; his ossuary indicates that the Romans honored Israelite tradition.

Following ancient practice, those who received Yochanan's crucified corpse bathed and anointed it, wrapping the body in linen and placing it in a funerary cave. According to usual burial practice, they deposited the bones in a limestone box after a year and carved Yochanan's name on the ossurary's side. This discovery directly contradicts the claim, fashionable for more than a century, that Jesus' body was tossed to the dogs after his execution. Foundational texts of Judaism give precise instructions for dealing with corpses after crucifixion; a dead body that was exposed was a source of impurity and offended God. Mary and her companions returned to Jesus' tomb in order to fulfill the Torah's commandment, having waited until sundown on the Sabbath so that they could buy materials for anointing Jesus' corpse. Modern readers often express disgust and incredulity at the thought of returning to a corpse that had already been interred for some thirty-six hours. But mourners in antiquity were not squeamish: Death had not yet been banished to the mortician's ghetto and anointing featured importantly in customs of burial in the ancient Near East.

Death's impurity had to be dealt with, and people accepted the temporary uncleanness of handling the corpse in order to ensure the purity of the land and the community of Israel.

The Talmud describes not only practices of cleaning, anointing, and wrapping the dead but also the custom of visiting the tomb each day for three days after a burial to make certain that the deceased was truly dead, not simply unconscious. The Talmud in question is the Babylonian Talmud (also called the Bavli), which is later than the Talmud of Jerusalem but nonetheless constitutes the pivotal text of Rabbinic Judaism. The story of the resuscitation of Lazarus in John 11:1-44 presupposes that custom. The Talmud speaks of people going on to lead healthy lives, as Lazarus did, when dedicated relatives and friends discovered they had, in fact, been interred alive. The moment of natural death can seem strangely uncertain, as anyone who has visited the terminally ill and their families knows. A woman once asked me to come to her home, unsure of whether cancer had at last claimed her husband's life. That kind of doubt is natural; the recovery of the supposedly dead sometimes defies medical technology. I gave the man last rites but stayed with his family until a medical practitioner could confirm his death.

Until then, the family lived through the same limbo that ancient Jewish mourners endured for three days—more in the case of Lazarus. This concern—to be sure a living person is not treated as dead—stems from a deep regard for life. In the ancient Israelite ethos, caring for a person extended to taking care of his body until the transition from life to death was complete. Crucifixion at the hands of the Romans left virtually no room for uncertainty over the fact of death and required the treatment of a badly damaged corpse. Puncture wounds leaked blood and lymphatic fluid, and bits of broken bone extruded; victims who had been flogged prior to crucifixion were covered with deep gashes. In Jesus' case, a javelin had also been thrust into his body.

The Roman Empire was in the business of death, using crucifixion as the supreme punishment to terrorize recalcitrant subjects in its dominions between Spain and Syria. They had learned this technique of state terror from the Persian Empire, then went on to master and monopolize it.

Crucifixion was a punishment that only the Roman authorities themselves— rather than their client kings or other petty rulers—could inflict. These executioners knew what they were doing, and theories that Jesus somehow physically survived the cross represent a combination of fantasy, revisionism, and half-baked science. The women did not go to the tomb to confirm that Jesus was dead, but to anoint and care for what they knew all too well was a corpse. The women had joined Joseph of Arimathea, a sympathetic rabbi who offered his own family's burial cave to be used for Jesus' interment (Mark 15:42-46). But the observance of the Sabbath (which arrived at sunset) prevented them from purchasing or preparing anointment at the time Jesus was buried. Their delay was therefore natural, calibrated to the rhythm of observant Judaism. To complete the dutiful care of their dead rabbi, Mary and the women made their way to the tomb. Perfumed oil for rubbing on the dead was scented with the resin of myrrh and the leaves of aloe . The astringent properties of the aloe helped to seal skin made porous by death. The smell of myrrh was associated in the mind of any dedicated Israelite with the aroma of the Temple. Both these scents were also used in the luxurious perfume that a lover might enjoy on the body of the beloved. Suspensions of myrrh and aloe were delicate mixtures, produced by seething them in oil and aging the unction in stone containers.

In the case of Jesus, a rabbi named Nicodemus saw to the expense so that Mary Magdalene and her companions could purchase the salve from a sympathetic vendor in Jerusalem, who was willing to make the sale as soon as the setting sun brought an end to the Sabbath. They bought their oil and spices so that they "could go anoint" the body of Jesus. To say they had to "go" for that purpose suggests they walked a distance; one ancient manuscript of the New Testament says they "proceeded", implying an even longer journey.

This choice of words embarrassed later copyists, who eliminated any reference to the women's travel because it contradicted the tradition that Jesus was buried in the Church of the Holy Sepulcher, one of Christianity's greatest pilgrimage (and hence tourist) sites since the fourth century. Modern archaeology has discredited the notion that this church is the site of Jesus' grave.

Mary Magdalene and her companions found Jesus' tomb in a recognized cemetery well outside the city—a place where prominent people, such as Joseph of Arimathea, purchased caves for family burial. The archaeological evidence for the existence of such sites is now secure. In 1990, on a hill dotted with natural caves in the Arab hamlet of Abu Tor, a mile and a half south of the Temple, the ossuary of Caiaphas, the high priest at the time of Jesus' execution, was discovered. There is little doubt whose ossuary this is: The limestone box was found in situ, with Caiaphas's name written on it twice. A coin discovered in the same cave bears the imprint of Herod Agrippa I, which shows that burial took place in the mid-forties of the first century. The carving on the box picks up the symbolism of the Temple, signaling Caiaphas's status as high priest. Was it in this cemetery that Joseph of Arimathea, a member of the same council to which the high priest belonged, interred the corpse of Jesus? Certainty escapes us, but it is clear that the women as described in Mark went to a private and remote place, much more like Abu Tor than the site of the Church of the Holy Sepulcher inside the city. Taking place well outside the city, far from earshot or the prying eyes of opponents, the experience at the mouth of the tomb was the women's alone.

The three women met there privately with Jesus, just as three men—Peter, James, and John—did on the mountain of the Transfiguration. In the experience of both female and male disciples, revelation came as a communal vision that intensified each individual's insight. Vision crystallized the women's conviction that Jesus was alive, a vibrant spiritual presence despite his shameful death. It was their Transfiguration.

Ancient Judaism conceived of visionary reality as an experience that could be shared—and it was this Transfiguration at the mouth of the tomb that emerged as the force that ultimately turned Jesus' movement into a new religion.

The Transfiguration and Jesus' Resurrection provoked astonishment and awe, highlighting the mystical qualities of encounters with the divine in Mark's Gospel. When Jesus performed an exorcism in the Capernaum synagogue, Mark describes the people there as "all were astonished." This scene establishes a clear pattern in the Gospel: astonishment and awe were a litmus test of revelation. The peasants of Galilee yearned for transformation into the Kingdom of God, which some rabbis of the time called ha-olam haba, or "the age to come," when the power of God's eternal Throne would transcend all divisions, heal all ills, and overpower the petty tyrannies of a broken world. Any experience or sign that offered a glimpse into this ultimate reality provoked awestruck joy.

Visionary prophets such as Ezekiel and mystical practitioners of Judaism after him conceived of this divine power as "the Chariot." The divine Chariot was nothing other than the Throne of God, which Moses and his companions (Aaron, Nadab, Abihu, and seventy elders of Israel) saw in its sapphire glory. Like the Resurrection of Jesus, the Chariot was open to communal vision and could unveil itself anywhere, anytime. Jewish texts from before, during, and after the first century show that rabbis practiced the unveiling of the Chariot in this world by means of disciplined meditation. Visions were not just spontaneous experiences that burst in on passive recipients; adepts could realize the Chariot through their dedicated practice.

Rabbi Jesus trained his disciples, including Mary Magdalene, in the tradition of the Merkavah, the Chariot, from the time she met him in Galilee through the period of his final pilgrimage to Jerusalem.

They attuned themselves to the divine Chariot, helped by Scriptures they memorized, disciplines they handed on by word of mouth, and examples of their master's teaching and practice that they emulated. Astonishment in God's presence became their way of life.

This astonishment strikes Peter, James, and John during the Transfiguration, when Jesus is transformed before them into a gleaming white figure. They see him speaking with Moses and Elijah, the two most powerful prophets of Israel's Scriptures. Jesus' visions began as his own personal revelations, but years of communal meditation made his experiences transparent to his disciples. On the mountain of his Transfiguration, Jesus followed in the footsteps of Moses, who took three of his followers (Aaron, Nadab, and Abihu) up Mount Sinai (Exodus 24:1-11), where they sacrificed and banqueted to celebrate their vision of the God of Israel on his sapphire Throne.

But unlike what happened on Sinai, Jesus' disciples, covered by a shining cloud of glory, also heard a voice: "This is my Son, the beloved, in whom I take pleasure: hear him." When the cloud passed, Moses and Elijah had disappeared. Jesus stood alone as God's Son. Divine "Son" was the designation that Jesus had heard when, as an adolescent, encamped on the River Jordan with his rabbi, John the Baptist, he had practiced mystical ascension; now his own disciples saw and heard the truth of his personal vision. Jesus' true genius lay in the transparency of his visionary experience.

When Jesus was immersed in the Spirit, the voice that came from heaven did not speak in the exclusive language of the later doctrine of the Trinity, which made Jesus into the only (and only possible) "Son of God." Rather, Jesus' immersion in Spirit enabled him to initiate others into that experience. Likewise, the voice from the luminous cloud in the Transfiguration signaled that the divine Spirit, which had animated Moses and Elijah, was present in Jesus and that Jesus could pass on that Spirit to his followers, each of whom could also become a child, or "Son," of God.

The whole Gospel According to Mark is designed as a program to train its hearers and readers for the moment of baptism, when they, too, will experience the Spirit within them and call upon God as their Abba, their father and true source.

Jesus knew that everyone's perceptions, including his own, had to change and adjust to this transcendent vision. As God's own Son, he was as confused as every Son who would ever follow the path he marked, taking up a cross and crossing over into the world of glory. This pattern of confusion in the face of revelation climaxes in Jesus' Resurrection. This experience manifested what theologians often refer to as the "presence" of God in this world, although the word "presence" scarcely conveys the inexhaustible dynamism of the Chariot, which welded human consciousness to God's as he founded the universe, maintained its precarious existence moment by moment, and was poised to sweep it all away at will.

Christianity became highly philosophical and often abstract from the second century onward, but Jesus and his Judaic contemporaries did not share the abstractions that have become common currency in the language of the divine world. For Rabbi Jesus, the word God conveyed not a philosophical idea but the ultimate reality—beautiful and fearsome and overpowering. At the mouth of the tomb, Mary Magdalene and her companions were taught definitively by Jesus that God was the only, ultimate truth—the omnipotent, swirling vortex of creation.

Although the Transfiguration itself and the vision of the women at the mouth of the tomb obviously reflect different experiences, both revealed Jesus' divine identity and thoroughly unnerved his disciples. Fear silenced the apostles on Mount Hebron, as though they were caught in a dream, unable to speak. Their silence prefigures the silence of the three women at the mouth of the tomb. In these cases, the disciples' astonishment signals a vision of the heavenly court, where the Chariot Throne of God is clouded in awe and radiates divine power.

Mark indicates that the women left our world and fearfully entered this realm. Both the Transfiguration and Mary's vision intimately connect Jesus to the Throne of God. In the Transfiguration, he appears in an altered form, shining in brilliance with Moses and Elijah, prophets who, it was understood in the first century, had "not tasted death," a turn of phrase shared among Jewish, Christian, and Gnostic texts. The phrase does not refer to escaping physical death, but to transcending its consequences. Vision gave access to a world where death no longer had dominion. Instead, dying marked an entry into God's presence.

The role of Mary Magdalene in the resurrection story is a topic of great significance in the study of the Gospels. The differences in how her story is presented in each of the four Gospels (Matthew, Mark, Luke, and John) reveal not only the unique styles and poetics of each Gospel but also provide insight into the early Christian communities who produced them.

The Gospel of Matthew, for instance, shows a break in the link between Mary's ritual anointing and Jesus' Resurrection. This attenuates her role, but an even deeper reduction in her importance, as compared to Mark, follows. Matthew undermines the women's vision at the tomb. Before describing Mary's experience with her colleagues, Matthew alludes to an earthquake that symbolizes Jesus' triumph over death. This legendary event appears only in Matthew's Gospel and has no historical source from the period. The scene in Matthew is no longer purely visionary, as it is in Mark, but a supernatural intervention into the physical world with tangible consequences. The women are completely passive, as if they were "as dead," like the guards.

Despite the differences, each Gospel is unique and develops a poetics all its own. Matthew was composed in Damascus, over a thousand miles away from Mark's Rome, in a city that Israel's prophets had long associated with the power of God's Spirit. In the years before there was any formal division between Judaism and Christianity, Jesus' followers saw their master as the fulfillment of Israel's destiny, and most of them worked out their peculiar vision in peace with their Jewish neighbors.

By the time Matthew's Gospel was written around 80 C.E., the leaders of churches in Damascus clearly saw themselves as separate from the synagogues there, and they stopped using the designation "rabbi" altogether. But Matthew also shows that the importance of vision had in no way diminished. This Gospel speaks of Jesus coming back to earth with his angels to judge all the nations, dividing them up into sheep and goats according to how people had behaved toward one another during their lives. Matthew's poetics pivot on the impact of apocalypse on the material world, just as Mark's poetics pivot on the silent amazement that revelation brings.

Despite sidelining Mary Magdalene's vision, Matthew does not completely erase her, any more than Mark did. This incomplete erasure underscores her pivotal role as the prime herald of Jesus' Resurrection. Matthew even admits what Mark only implies: after her angelic vision, Mary actually encounters the risen Jesus. Matthew's women not only see the angel, but they also meet Jesus himself as they depart from the mouth of the tomb. Matthew spells out what Mark implies—that the story of the women at the mouth of the tomb points toward a later encounter with Jesus himself.

The importance of physical reality in Luke's Gospel is even more pronounced. Luke has Mary and her companions search the tomb and find it empty. Likewise, Luke has the risen Jesus insist on his own physical reality. Only in this Gospel does Jesus explicitly say, "See my hands and my feet, that I am myself. Feel me and see, because a spirit does not have flesh and bone just as you perceive I have." Jesus even eats some fish to prove that his Resurrection is substantial and material. Despite this, in Luke's Gospel, Mary's vision becomes a brutal suppression. Mary Magdalene's whole orientation subverted Luke's materialism, and the women's testimony is dismissed as "nonsense" by the male disciples.

For Luke's Gospel, only Jesus personally, raised from the dead in flesh and bone, can explain his resurrected presence among his disciples.

The Gospel of John presents Mary Magdalene as the first person to witness the Resurrection. She is shown to be a central figure who has a significant role in the early Christian community. John's Gospel presents Mary as a figure of great faith and devotion to Jesus, who is rewarded with a vision of the risen Christ. In John's Gospel, Mary is the first person to see Jesus after his Resurrection, and she is the one who announces the good news to the disciples. Luke's Gospel indirectly references Mary's understanding of Jesus' practice of exorcism (8:2), as previously mentioned. However, this does not make the Gospel feminist because mentioning women is not the same as including them as active agents in Jesus' ministry and Resurrection. Luke utilized sources that apparently conveyed women's perspectives, but the Gospel itself maintains a different viewpoint that focuses on the unique authority of male apostles in Jerusalem.

When Luke presents a woman named Mary as choosing "the good part" of being a disciple by sitting at Jesus' feet instead of serving him, the Gospel takes care to clarify that this is Mary, Martha's sister, not Mary Magdalene. This ensures that the woman is not associated with any tradition or source that could rival the apostolic authority in Jerusalem. She doesn't even speak. Nevertheless, Jesus' mother, who is addressed by the angel Gabriel, identifies herself as "the slave of the Lord". Luke's dedication to the hierarchy of the Jerusalem apostles, combined with a view of the Resurrection that is, in its own way, as materialistic as Matthew's, resulted in the marginalization of the Magdalene, her vision, her source, and her practice of anointing.

In conclusion, the different portrayals of Mary Magdalene's role in the Resurrection story in the four Gospels reflect the unique styles and poetics of each Gospel and provide insight into the communities that produced them. While there are differences in the portrayal of Mary Magdalene, her importance as a witness to the Resurrection remains consistent throughout the Gospels.

Chapter Bonus Introduction

Mary Magdalene is a prominent figure in the Christian Canon and non-canonical gospels, with her name mentioned and identified several times in the Gospels of Mark, Matthew, Luke, and John. This confirms her presence and significance among Biblical women. Furthermore, in several of the books, Jesus appears first to Mary following his resurrection. Despite her distinctions over practically all other women, she is only mentioned eleven times in the Gospels (two chapters each). This contrast between Mary Magdalene's obvious grandeur and the scarcity of her mention appears to be a remarkable oddity, hinting to hidden purposes and implications.

In the Gospel of Mark, Mary Magdalene is first mentioned in chapter 15:40. In this verse, she is with a group of women who are "looking on from afar" as the crucifixion of Jesus takes place. The reason for this is not explained, but it can be assumed that women were not permitted to attend such sessions or that the women did not want to face persecution for associating with Jesus. Regardless, three critical insights are provided. The ladies were Jesus' disciples who "followed him and ministered to him," according to the Bible. Furthermore, Mary Magdalene is listed first among these women disciples, emphasizing her favor not only among women, but also among disciples. Finally, and maybe purposefully, the passage affirms Mary as a firsthand witness to the crucifixion, which will become more relevant momentarily.

The presence of Mary Magdalene is highlighted next in a one sentence section. According to Mark 15:47, Mary Magdalene, who was listed first in the company of Mary, the mother of Joses, "saw where he was laid." The austerity of this section emphasizes two elements about Mary Magdalene in the text: her superiority over her friends and her presence at the burial.

In Mark 16:1, Mary Magdalene is on her way to Jesus' tomb with many other women to anoint his body with spices. She is the only figure in Mark who is mentioned at the crucifixion, burial, and resurrection, and she is again identified first. The tomb was empty when the women arrived, except for a young man dressed in white who informed them that Jesus had risen. Despite the youth's commands to tell Jesus' followers, the women fled in terror and astonishment, not telling anyone about the resurrection (Mark 16:8). However, in 16:9, Mary Magdalene has a post-resurrection vision of Jesus, after which she tells the Apostles about the resurrection. Until Jesus appears to the men, her account is regarded with skepticism.

Mark 16's depiction of Mary Magdalene is noteworthy for a variety of reasons. Her significance is stressed countless times over. In addition to the pattern of first mention, she is the first figure to view (and probably speak to) Jesus following his resurrection, before any of the male disciples. Furthermore, she is the messenger of his resurrection to the men, which suggests he chose her over all others to carry this word. Furthermore, Mary is the sole witness to all three key Passion scenes. Finally, the women are described as "trembling" and "afraid," and Mary as "from whom he [Jesus] had cast out seven demons." These descriptions show the entire group of ladies, including Mary, to be terrified and so weak.

In Luke 8:2, Mary Magdalene is first introduced as one of the women who had been healed of evil spirits and infirmities by Jesus, and who had also been supporting him out of their own means. This passage not only establishes Mary Magdalene's association with Jesus and her status as a believer, but also emphasizes her generosity and dedication to him.

As the story of Jesus' crucifixion and resurrection unfolds in Luke, Mary Magdalene is again highlighted as a prominent figure. In Luke 23:55, she is mentioned as one of the women who had followed Jesus from Galilee and were present at the crucifixion, along with other women and the male disciples. This passage confirms her presence as a witness to the crucifixion, and her role as a follower of Jesus.

In the following chapter, Luke 24:1-10, Mary Magdalene, along with other women, is again the first to arrive at the tomb on the first day of the week and is the first to find it empty. They are also the first to encounter the angels who tell them of Jesus' resurrection. In this passage, Mary Magdalene is once again emphasized as the first and foremost among the women, and as a key witness to the events of the resurrection.

Furthermore, in Luke 24:10, Mary Magdalene is the first person to report the empty tomb and the news of the resurrection to the male disciples, and they initially do not believe her. This further highlights her significance as a messenger of the resurrection, and as a key figure in the early Christian community.

Overall, Mary Magdalene is presented as a prominent and significant figure throughout the Gospels, particularly in the accounts of the crucifixion and resurrection. She is consistently mentioned first among the women and is a key witness to the events of these crucial moments in Jesus' life and in the history of Christianity. Her presence as a disciple, a supporter, a witness, and a messenger of the resurrection, and her prominence as a figure in the early Christian community, all serve to emphasize her significance in the Biblical narrative.

Personality

In early Christian literature, Mary Magdalene is depicted as a prominent Jewish disciple of Jesus of Nazareth. Her name "Magdalene" likely refers to the town of Magdala, which is located on the west side of the Sea of Galilee. She is seen as a key figure in the gospels and is often portrayed as one of the first to see and communicate with the risen Lord. In some texts, such as the Gospel of Thomas and the First Apocalypse of James, she is shown as having a special bond with Jesus and is praised for her spiritual understanding. Despite this, there are indications that her portrayal as a model disciple was not necessarily associated with a positive representation of women in general. In some texts, such as the Pistis Sophia, there is a conflict between Mary and the male disciples, particularly Peter, with her being accused of misogyny. However, the text ultimately asserts that sex and gender have no bearing on spiritual growth, and anyone infused with the Spirit of light has the capacity and obligation to speak.

One of the most interesting aspects of Mary Magdalene's character is the way she is portrayed in early Christian literature. In some texts, such as the Gospel of Luke, she is depicted as a repentant sinner who is forgiven by Jesus. In other texts, such as the Gospel of John, she is portrayed as a devoted follower of Jesus who is present at his crucifixion and is the first person to see him after his resurrection.

In addition to her role as a disciple, Mary Magdalene is also often depicted as a leader among the women who followed Jesus. For example, in the Gospel of Thomas, she is one of only five disciples mentioned by name, and she is the one who asks Jesus a question. This suggests that she played a significant role in the early Christian community and was respected for her spiritual understanding.

However, it's also important to note that Mary Magdalene's portrayal in early Christian literature was not always positive. In some texts, such as the Gospel of Matthew, there are indications that she was a source of controversy and conflict within the early Christian community. For example, in Matthew, Peter is shown rejecting Mary because she is a woman, and Jesus is depicted as defending her spiritual standing.

This suggests that there was some debate within the early Christian community about the role of women and their spiritual capabilities. However, it's important to note that these texts also emphasize that gender and sex have no bearing on spiritual growth and that anyone, regardless of their gender, can attain spiritual understanding if they are "infused with the Spirit of light."

In the centuries that followed, Mary Magdalene was the subject of many legends and stories, many of which portrayed her as a powerful and enlightened spiritual figure. Some of these stories depicted her as a teacher and healer who traveled throughout the Mediterranean spreading the teachings of Jesus. Others portrayed her as a powerful prophetess who was able to perform miracles and had a special connection to the divine.

As a result of these legends, Mary Magdalene became an important figure in various Christian traditions, particularly in the Gnostic and Eastern Orthodox traditions. In these traditions, she is often venerated as a saint and is considered to be an important spiritual guide and mentor.

Overall, Mary Magdalene is a fascinating and complex figure in early Christian literature. Her portrayal in the texts varies, but they all seem to agree that she played a significant role in the early Christian community and was respected for her spiritual understanding.

Mary Gospel teachings

The Gospel of Mary is an apocryphal text that was discovered in Egypt in the late 19th century. It is believed to have been written in the 2nd century, around the same time as the New Testament gospels. The text is a gnostic gospel, which means that it presents a form of Christianity that emphasizes inner spiritual transformation and the acquisition of secret knowledge.

The main theme of the Gospel of Mary is the teachings of Jesus as a teacher and mediator of divine revelation. The text presents Jesus as a savior who reveals the truth about the nature of the human soul and the path to eternal life with God. According to the text, Jesus teaches that at death, the body dissolves into the elements out of which it came, but the spiritual soul is immortal and lives forever. He also teaches that people are spiritual beings made in the image of God, and that the goal of salvation is not the resurrection of the body at the end of the age, but the ascent of the soul to God.

The teachings in the Gospel of Mary differ significantly from those found in other Christian texts. For example, the text does not emphasize the death and resurrection of Jesus as the core of Christian belief, but rather as the occasion for the disciples' mission to preach the gospel. The text also portrays God as simply the Good and not as a wrathful ruler or judge. Additionally, the text does not include concepts such as hell and eternal punishment.

The Gospel of Mary was likely written by a group of early Christians who were heavily influenced by ancient Greek and Roman philosophy and piety. They likely drew on popular philosophical ideas and pieties to interpret the teachings of Jesus. The text reflects a stream of Christianity that was different from the dominant orthodoxy of the time, which emphasized the fulfillment of Hebrew scripture and the separation of Christians from Jews.

It is important to note that the Gospel of Mary was not accepted as part of the canon of the New Testament, and it was not considered to be authoritative by the early Church. Being a gnostic gospel, it was rejected as heretical by the early Church. Despite this, the text continues to be of interest to scholars and researchers for the insights it provides into the diversity of early Christianity and the different ways in which Jesus' teachings were interpreted by different groups of Christians.

Mary's teaching is broken down into-

1. The body and the world: In the Gospel of Mary, the material world is seen as a source of evil and temptation, with the body being a prison for the soul. This idea is similar to the Platonic belief that the material world is a shadow of the true reality and that the body is a hindrance to the soul's ascent to the Divine Realm. However, in the Gospel of Mary, the emphasis is placed on the need for correct knowledge of Reality to free the soul from the influence of the passions, rather than the Platonic idea of the soul's innate knowledge of the Good.

2. Sin, judgment and law: In the Gospel of Mary, the concept of sin is closely tied to the influence of the passions and the material world on the soul. The idea of judgment and law, as found in the Jewish tradition, is also present, but with a different emphasis. Instead of being punished for breaking the law, the soul is judged based on its conformity with the pattern of the Good. This idea is similar to the Stoic belief that the goal of life is to live in accordance with nature and reason.

3. The Son of Man: In the Gospel of Mary, the Son of Man is presented as a spiritual guide and teacher who helps the soul to attain correct knowledge of Reality and ascend to the Divine Realm. This idea is similar to the Platonic concept of the philosopher-king, who leads the soul to the Good. However, in the Gospel of Mary, the emphasis is placed on the need for personal experience and spiritual transformation, rather than on the acquisition of knowledge.

4. The rise of the soul: In the Gospel of Mary, the ascent of the soul to the Divine Realm at death is presented as the ultimate goal of human existence. This idea is similar to the Platonic and Stoic belief in the immortality of the soul and its eventual return to the Divine Realm. However, in the Gospel of Mary, the emphasis is placed on the role of correct knowledge and spiritual transformation in achieving this goal, rather than on the soul's innate nature or reason.

In conclusion, the ideas found in the Gospel of Mary can be seen as a blending of the Platonic, Stoic, and Jesus traditions. While it shares similarities with these philosophies, the Gospel of Mary develops its thinking out of the Jesus tradition, which made an enormous difference in both its theological content and social dynamics. Understanding these confluences can help us to grasp the significance of these ideas and how they were understood in early Christian communities.

The body and the world

The body and the world are two integral parts of our existence, and the relationship between them has been a topic of philosophical debate for centuries. The Gospel of Mary offers a unique perspective on this relationship, framing it within the context of a dialogue between the Savior and his disciples. The dialogue begins with a question from one of the disciples about the nature of the material universe: "Will matter then be utterly destroyed or not?" The Savior responds by stating that all material things are interconnected and have no ultimate spiritual value and that in the end, they will dissolve back into their original condition, which he calls their "root."

This question and answer reflect the influence of contemporary philosophical debates about whether the matter is preexistent or created. If the matter is preexistent, then it is eternal; if it is created, then it is subject to destruction. Only a few early philosophers, such as Eudorus of Alexandria, held that matter was created out of nothing, although this position later became widely accepted.

A more common position for the early period is reported by Cicero when he discusses the Platonists: "But they hold that underlying all things is a substance called 'matter,' entirely formless and devoid of all 'quality,'... and that out of it all things have been formed and produced, so that this matter can in its totality receive all things and undergo every sort of transformation throughout every part of it, and in fact even suffers dissolution, not into nothingness but into its own parts."

This concept presumes that matter has no form or qualities of its own; it is simply the substratum that is subject to being formed or produced. The Savior agrees with this concept and states that everything will dissolve back into its own proper root. It does not matter whether things occur by nature, whether they have been molded out of formlessness, or whether they have been created from nothing, all will return to their original condition.

He doesn't take a clear position on whether that natural state is formlessness or nothingness, but either way, his point is clear: "anyone with two ears" should realize that because the material realm is entirely destined for dissolution, it is temporary, and therefore the world and the body have no ultimate spiritual value.

For both Plato and the Gospel of Mary, there are two natures, one belonging to the material world and one to the Divine Realm. Evil belongs only in the material world and is associated with the finite and changing character of material reality. The nature of the Divine Realm is perfect Goodness, unchanging and eternal. The material world is the place of suffering and death; the Divine Realm offers immortality in peace. The dualism between the material and the Divine is definitely sharper in the Gospel of Mary than in Plato, but we should not exaggerate it. The Savior argues that the material world is destined to dissolve back into its original root-nature; he does not say that it is evil and will be destroyed.

The position that the world is fleeting is hardly new to Christian thought. Paul had written that "the form of this world is passing away," and the Gospel of Mark says that "heaven and earth will pass away." However, the difference between these traditional Christian views and the perspective presented in the Gospel of Mary is in the understanding of what happens after the dissolution of the material world. In the traditional Christian view, the dissolution of the material world is seen as the prelude to a new creation, a new world in which righteousness dwells and believers will live eternally with God. But in the Gospel of Mary, there is no mention of a new creation. The dissolution of the material world is understood as the final state when everything that is now mixed up together will be separated and return to its proper "root" - the material to its formless nature or nothingness, and the spiritual to its root in the Good.

This understanding of the ultimate fate of the world is closely tied to ethics, as it raises the question of how one should live in the face of the fleeting nature of the material world. The book of 2 Peter addresses this question directly, stating that "what sort of person ought you to be in lives of holiness and godliness, waiting for and hastening the coming of the day of God, because of which the heavens will be kindled and dissolved, and the elements will melt with fire!" In other words, the understanding that the material world is temporary and ultimately destined for dissolution should inspire us to live a life of holiness and godliness, as we look forward to the day when all things will be made right.

The Gospel of Mary also presents a sharper dualism between the material and the Divine realm than is found in Plato. According to the Gospel, the material world is the place of suffering and death, while the Divine realm offers immortality in peace. Evil belongs only in the material world and is associated with the finite and changing character of material reality. The nature of the Divine realm is perfect Goodness, unchanging and eternal.

However, it is important to note that the Savior in the Gospel of Mary does not state that the material world is evil and will be destroyed. Instead, he argues that the material world is destined to dissolve back into its original root nature. This understanding of the material world as temporary and ultimately insignificant in the grand scheme of things should inspire us to focus on the truly important things in life - living a life of holiness and godliness and striving for spiritual fulfillment in the Divine realm.

In conclusion, the understanding of the ultimate fate of the world presented in the Gospel of Mary is unique in its rejection of the idea of a new creation and its emphasis on the dissolution of the material world as the final state. This perspective raises important ethical questions about how we should live our lives in light of the fleeting nature of the material world. It also presents a sharper dualism between the material and the Divine realm than is found in Plato, emphasizing the temporary and insignificant nature of the material world in comparison to the eternal and unchanging nature of the Divine realm.

Sin, Judgement, and law

The Gospel of Mary, a non-canonical Christian text, defines sin differently from traditional Christian theology, which understands sin as the condition of human estrangement from God. In the Gospel of Mary, the Savior is primarily concerned with orienting the soul towards God and defines sin as the mixing of the spiritual and material natures. The material world cannot be the basis for determining good and evil, right and wrong, as it will eventually dissolve. The sinfulness of the human condition is caused by attachment to the material world, which leads to a fatal love of perishable material nature, the source of disturbing passions, physical suffering, and death. The Good came to humanity to establish people in their true nature and set them up firmly within their proper "root," the natural good within themselves. The Savior goes on to develop the distinction between matter and true nature, relying on the Platonic distinction between the changeable material world and the immutable world of Ideas. Passion "has no Image" in the immutable Divine Realm, because it is not a true reflection of anything in the immutable Divine Realm and is contrary to the true nature of spiritual Reality. People suffer because they are led by the unnatural and deceptive passions of the body. Peace of heart can be found only by turning away from the material world and focusing on the spiritual self.

One important aspect to note is that the Gospel of Mary does not adhere to the traditional Christian doctrine of original sin, which posits that all humans are inherently sinful due to the actions of Adam and Eve in the Garden of Eden. Instead, the text presents a more Gnostic perspective in which the human soul is fundamentally pure and good but is trapped in a material body that is prone to deception and passion. In this sense, the sin of the world is not a moral or legal transgression, but rather a state of ignorance and separation from one's true spiritual nature. The Savior's message in the Gospel of Mary is primarily focused on guiding the soul towards enlightenment and union with God, rather than emphasizing the need for repentance and forgiveness of sins.

Additionally, the text also emphasizes the idea that matter is ultimately transient and inferior to the spiritual realm, and that the ultimate goal of the human being is to transcend the material world and return to their true spiritual nature. This is reflected in the Savior's statement that "matter will be dissolved" and that "those who are exalted above the world will not be dissolved, for they are eternal" (GPhil 53:17-23).

In this way, the Gospel of Mary presents a unique and divergent view of sin and the nature of the human being compared to orthodox Christian theology. It emphasizes the importance of spiritual enlightenment and transcendence over moral rules and regulations and posits that the true self is not the material body, but rather the soul infused with the spirit.

The Son of Man

The Coptic phrase "rrcyHpe SnpcuMe", commonly translated as "Son of Man," holds a significant meaning in the Gospel of Mary. In this gospel, the "Son of Man" represents the child of true humanity and the image of the divine realm that resides within every person. It is seen as the true representation of humanity's spiritual nature and the ideal to which the disciples should aspire. The Savior tells the disciples that "The child of true humanity exists within you" and commands them to "follow it! Those who search for it will find it".

The idea of following the child of true humanity requires identifying with the archetypal image of humanity and conforming to it as a model. This is in contrast to the interpretation of the "Son of Man" as a messianic figure in other gospel works, such as the Gospel of Mark, where the "Son of Man" is seen as a figure who will come with power and glory in the end times. The Gospel of Mary warns against being deceived by such claims and instead emphasizes that the true self, represented by the "Son of Man," can only be found within.

The "Son of Man" in the Gospel of Mary also has roots in Platonic philosophy, where the existence of a Form of Man in the divine realm apart from particular humans was posited. The gospel interprets Jesus' teachings on the child of true humanity to refer to this archetypal form of man, in connection with the creation story in Genesis 1:26-27, where humanity is created in the image of God.

In the Gospel of Mary, the Savior uses the generic term "human being" and makes both Mary and the male disciples into human beings. In contrast, the Gospel of Thomas uses the non-generic term "male" and speaks of making Mary male, suggesting a belief in male superiority. However, the Gospel of Mary strives to articulate a vision of a non-gendered divine and transcendent image, with sex and gender being seen as temporary and belonging to the lower sphere of bodily existence.

The divine, in this gospel, is seen as nonmaterial and nongendered, represented only by the Good, a term that can easily be grammatically neuter. Conforming to the divine image, therefore, requires abandoning distinctions, including sex and gender, and embracing the spiritual and nongendered nature of the true self.

The rise of the soul

Mary recounts the Savior's teachings about the soul's journey through four Powers who seek to keep it bound to the material world. The first Power is assumed to be Darkness, but the text picks up with the second Power, Desire, challenging the soul's right to ascend. Desire claims that the soul belongs to the material world, but the soul exposes the Power's ignorance by revealing that the body is merely a garment, not the true self. The soul then ascends to the third Power, Ignorance, which questions its origin and motives. But the soul confidently asserts its freedom from the material bonds, its superiority in recognizing the true nature of things, and its return to its place of origin above. The soul then encounters the fourth Power, Wrath, which accuses it of violence, but the soul happily embraces these terms as evidence of its victory over the material elements. The soul finds rest in silence and ascends to a timeless realm, contrasting mortality with immortality and the deceptive image below with the true Image above. The author of the Apocalypse of Paul draws upon similar teachings, but expands on the journey of the soul, imagining and describing all that it encounters.

The author of the Apocalypse of Paul uses the story of Paul's journey to the heavens as a framework for their own revelation of the soul's ascent to God. In the text, the soul encounters four Powers that seek to keep it bound to the material world. The first of these is Darkness, followed by Desire, Ignorance, and finally Wrath. The soul, however, is wise and playful, and is able to overcome these Powers and ascend to its true spiritual home. The ascent of the soul is a central theme in many ancient cultures and religious traditions, and the author of the Apocalypse of Paul uses this motif to convey their own spiritual insights.

The author also draws on the tradition of the Oracle of Apollo at Claros, where someone asked Apollo about the fate of the soul after death. The oracle answered that the soul, as long as it is bound to the mortal body, is subject to the pains of that body. But once the body dies and the soul is set free, it is borne to the ether and forever abides untroubled.

The author combines these traditional themes with their own creative imagination to craft a unique vision of the soul's journey to God. They reveal everything they saw and heard during their own spiritual journey, imagining the third heaven as just the beginning of the soul's ascent. At the fourth heaven, they see angels whipping a soul who had been brought out of the land of the dead. The author's vivid descriptions of the soul's encounters with the Powers and their journey to God serve to inspire the reader and encourage them to strive for their own spiritual liberation.

The journey of the soul continues as it ascends to higher and higher levels of spiritual enlightenment and knowledge. Beyond the third Power of Ignorance, the soul encounters the fourth Power of Death. Again, the soul is challenged and questioned, but remains steadfast and true to its path of enlightenment and ascension. The fourth Power tries to keep the soul bound to the material world, to keep it tied to the cycle of birth and death, but the soul's wisdom and strength are too great, and it rises up and overcomes Death's grasp.

As the soul continues to rise, it encounters the fifth Power of Flesh, which represents the physical body and its base desires and needs. The fifth Power tries to keep the soul tied to the material world through temptation and desire, but the soul remains strong and refuses to be tempted. The soul recognizes that the desires of the flesh are temporary and illusory, and instead focuses on its spiritual journey and the higher truths that it is seeking.

The sixth Power, Foolishness, also tries to keep the soul bound to the material world. This Power represents the ignorance and confusion that often comes from living in the material world, and it tries to convince the soul that the world of matter is all there is, that there is no higher truth or spiritual reality. However, the soul remains steadfast in its wisdom and knowledge, and it rises up and overcomes Foolishness.

Finally, the soul reaches the seventh Power, Wrath, which represents the anger and violence that are inherent in the material world. The seventh Power tries to keep the soul tied to the world of matter through fear and intimidation, but the soul remains unshaken, and it rises up and overcomes Wrath as well. With each Power that the soul overcomes, it becomes more and more enlightened, and its journey brings it closer and closer to the divine.

Ultimately, the soul reaches a state of pure spiritual enlightenment, a state of pure understanding and union with the divine. This state is called "the First-born Divine Providence," and it represents the ultimate destination of the soul's journey. Here, the soul finds rest and peace, forever immune from the pains and tribulations of the material world.

And so, the story of the soul's journey to God is a tale of spiritual enlightenment and the triumph of the human spirit over the limitations and hardships of the material world. Through its journey, the soul learns to recognize the higher truths and to reject the illusions and temptations of the material world. In the end, the soul finds its true place in the divine realm, and it is able to rest in peace and unity with the divine.

Pistis Sophia

Introduction

"Pistis Sophia" is a Gnostic text that is believed to have been written in Egypt during the 2nd or 3rd century AD. The text is considered one of the most important works of Gnosticism, a religious and philosophical movement that emerged in the early Christian era. The term "Gnosticism" comes from the Greek word "gnosis" which means "knowledge" or "insight". Gnostics believed that they possessed a special kind of knowledge that allowed them to achieve a closer relationship with the divine and escape the cycle of reincarnation.

The "Pistis Sophia" describes the journey of the soul towards divine wisdom and presents a complex mythology that blends elements of Christianity, Greek philosophy, and oriental mysticism. The text is structured as a dialogue between Jesus and his disciples, in which Jesus imparts his teachings to them. It covers a wide range of topics including the creation of the world, the nature of the divine, and the fate of the soul after death.

One of the key themes in "Pistis Sophia" is the concept of the divine spark within each person. Gnostics believed that the divine spark was present within all people and could be awakened through the acquisition of gnosis. The text also emphasizes the role of the divine feminine, including Sophia, the personification of wisdom, and the Holy Spirit, who is portrayed as a feminine being.

The text was widely read and studied by Gnostic communities and had a significant influence on early Christian thought.

Some of the ideas and concepts presented in "Pistis Sophia" were later incorporated into other Gnostic texts, such as the "Apocryphon of John" and the "Thunder, Perfect Mind". However, the text was eventually suppressed by the early Christian church, which considered Gnosticism to be a heretical movement.

Today, "Pistis Sophia" is considered a valuable historical document that sheds light on the diversity of early Christian beliefs and practices. The text remains an important source of information for scholars studying the development of Gnosticism and the early Christian movement.

The First Book of Sophia

Jesus spent 11 years instructing his disciples, teaching them about the First Mystery and the First Commandment. The disciples believed the First Mystery was the head of the universe and all existence and that it was the completion of all things. However, Jesus had not told his disciples about the total expansion of all regions, including the emanations of the great Invisible, the Treasury of the Light, and their orders, the regions of the three Amēns, the five Trees, the seven Voices, the five Helpers, the five Impressions, and the First Commandment. He had only taught them generally so they were not aware of the existence of other regions within the mystery. The disciples thought the First Mystery was the completion of completions and the head of the universe because Jesus said that it surrounded the universe he had been speaking of.

One day, the disciples sat on the Mount of Olives, discussing joyful words and praising the Savior for revealing the fullness to them. On the full moon, a powerful light appeared behind the sun and descended upon Jesus, enveloping him completely. The light was too bright for the disciples to see Jesus and only saw the rays of light, each one more brilliant than the next, stretching from earth to heaven. The sight of the light filled the disciples with fear and agitation.

Jesus descended from heaven in an immense light and the powers of heaven, along with the disciples and people of the world, were in chaos and agitation. The disciples were afraid and wept until Jesus comforted them, saying "It is I, be not afraid."

The disciples then fell down and worshiped him, asking about his journey and the events that had taken place. Jesus revealed that he had been to the regions he had come from and that he would speak openly with the disciples from that point forward, revealing all truths and mysteries. He had sat on the Mount of Olives to reflect on the completion of his mission and the mysteries he was to reveal.

Jesus continued his discourse with his disciples, saying that he had received powers from various entities and cast them into the world and into people. He then said that the time had come for him to put on his vesture and receive full authority. He would reveal all mysteries to his disciples, and nothing would be hidden from them. He spoke of a great light power that came down and in which his vesture was found. The vesture was written in five words, and its solution was a call to the First Mystery, who was the source of all emanations, to come to them as they were all part of the same entity. They called Jesus to put on the vesture and be clothed with the First Mystery and its glory.

A great light caused all the æons and heavens to become agitated and all the tyrants to fight in vain. Then, Jesus took a third of their power, changed their Fate and sphere, and set them to face the left and right six months at a time, so they could no longer accomplish evil deeds. Mary Magdalene asked permission to speak and received it from Jesus, who praised her for being blessed above all women. She spoke about a prophecy from the prophet Isaiah that spoke of the power of the Lord Sabaōth, and Jesus praised her for her words. Mary then fell down before Jesus and asked to question him before he spoke further.

Philip asked Jesus why he changed the path of the rulers of the æons and their fate, and Jesus explained that it was for the salvation of all souls. Without his intervention, many souls would have been destroyed and the completion of the perfect souls would have been delayed.

Philip asked Jesus why he changed the path of the rulers of the æons and their fate. Jesus explained that it was for the salvation of all souls. Without his intervention, many souls would have been destroyed and the completion of the perfect souls would have been delayed. Mary asks how the souls would have delayed themselves, and Jesus explains that the rulers of the æons and the fate were bound in their bonds and their spheres. When the time of Melchisedec, the great Receiver of the Light came, he carried away the purification of the light from the rulers and set in motion the hastener to make them turn their circles swiftly. When the rulers became powerless and their power ceased, their kingdom was destroyed and the universe was quickly raised up. When the number of the cipher of Melchisedec came, he threw the rulers into agitation and made them abandon their circles.

The disciples were amazed at the words of Jesus and asked for clarification on the completion of the perfect souls. Jesus explained that the perfect souls are those who have received the fullness of the light and have been purified from all their bonds and spheres. These souls have received the completion of their mysteries and have become part of the great Invisible. He said that these souls will receive eternal life and that their kingdom will not be destroyed, as it is bound to the Treasury of Light.

The disciples were filled with joy and asked for more information on the completion of the perfect souls. Jesus revealed that the completion of the perfect souls is only possible through the gift of the Holy Spirit, which is the source of all life and power. He said that those who receive the Holy Spirit will have the ability to overcome all their bonds and spheres and that they will be able to receive the completion of their mysteries.

The disciples asked Jesus to explain the Holy Spirit, and he revealed that it is the power of the great Invisible, which is the source of all the emanations. He said that the Holy Spirit is the completion of the perfect souls and the head of the universe. That those who receive the Holy Spirit will be able to understand all mysteries and receive the fullness of the light. That the Holy Spirit is the source of all life and power, and that it will never be destroyed.

Jesus continued his discourse, saying that the time had come for all souls to receive the Holy Spirit and to be purified from their bonds and spheres. He said that all souls have the ability to receive the Holy Spirit, and that it is up to them to choose whether they will receive it or not. He said that those who receive the Holy Spirit will have eternal life, and that their kingdom will not be destroyed, as it is bound to the Treasury of Light.

The disciples were filled with joy and asked Jesus to give them the Holy Spirit. Jesus said that he would give them the Holy Spirit, but that they must first be purified from their bonds and spheres. He said that they must be baptized in his name and receive the gift of the Holy Spirit in order to receive the fullness of the light and the completion of their mysteries. The disciples asked Jesus to baptize them, and he did so, giving them the gift of the Holy Spirit and the completion of their mysteries.

From that day forward, the disciples went out into the world, spreading the message of Jesus and the gift of the Holy Spirit. They baptized many people in the name of Jesus and gave them the gift of the Holy Spirit, bringing salvation to all those who received it.

Sophia's Story

"It came to pass then, that after Pistis Sophia had cried out in repentance, the First Commandment sent forth a ray of light from the Treasury of the Light. This ray of light reached down to Sophia and brought her back to her own region, the thirteenth æon. And the ray of light divided itself into three parts and surrounded her, and the three parts of the light remained in Sophia, and became a power in her, which is the three powers of the light that were to be given to the Saviour, who was to come into the world.

And Pistis Sophia, after she had been surrounded by the three parts of the light, gave birth to a perfect androgynous being, who was the first to come forth from her. This being was the first to become perfect in the three regions of the thirteenth æon, the region of all her brethren the invisible. And he was called by the name Christ, and he was the first to receive the power of the light which was in Pistis Sophia.

And after Christ had received the power of the light, Pistis Sophia also gave birth to a great power, who was to be the Lord of the æons, and he was called Sabaoth. And Sabaoth received the power of the light which was in Pistis Sophia, and he was to be the Lord of the æons, in the place of the rulers of the twelve æons, who were below Pistis Sophia.

It came to pass then, after Christ and Sabaoth had received the power of the light, that Pistis Sophia gave birth to another great power, who was to be the chief of the forces of the chaos, and he was called Adonaios.

And Adonaios received the power of the light which was in Pistis Sophia, and he was to be the chief of the forces of the chaos, in the place of the great triple-powered Self-willed, who had caused Pistis Sophia to fall into the chaos.

And after Adonaios had received the power of the light, Pistis Sophia also gave birth to another great power, who was to be the chief of the thirteenth æon, and he was called Iao. And Iao received the power of the light which was in Pistis Sophia, and he was to be the chief of the thirteenth æon, in the place of the rulers of the twelve æons, who were below Pistis Sophia.

And after Iao had received the power of the light, Pistis Sophia gave birth to a host of other powers, who were to be the guardians of the thirteenth æon, and they received the power of the light which was in Pistis Sophia. And these powers were to be the guardians of the thirteenth æon, in the place of the guards who were at the gates of the æons, who had hated Pistis Sophia.

And after all the powers had received the power of the light, Pistis Sophia returned to her own region, the thirteenth æon, and remained there. And she gave the three powers of the light to the Saviour, who was to come into the world, and she remained in the thirteenth æon, performing the mysteries of the light and singing praises to the light of the height, which she had seen in the light of the veil of the Treasury of the Light."

It came to pass then, when Jesus had finished speaking these words unto his disciples, that he said unto them: "Do ye understand in what manner I discourse with you?" And the disciples looked at each other, trying to grasp the full meaning of what Jesus had said. But then Peter stepped forward and spoke up.

"My Lord, we will not endure this woman, for she taketh the opportunity from us and hath let none of us speak, but she discourseth many times," Peter said.

Jesus replied, "Let him in whom the power of his spirit shall seethe, so that he understandeth what I say, come forward and speak. But now, Peter, I see thy power in thee, that it understandeth the solution of the mystery of the repentance which Pistis Sophia hath uttered. Now, therefore, Peter, speak the thought of her repentance in the midst of thy brethren."

And so, Peter spoke. He spoke of the words of the seventy-seventh Psalm, where the repentant soul cried out to God for deliverance and refuge from the evil ones who sought to destroy her. "This then is the solution of the second repentance which Pistis Sophia hath uttered," Peter declared.

Jesus nodded in approval. "Finely, Peter; this is the solution of her repentance. Blessed are ye before all men on the earth, because I have revealed unto you these mysteries. Amēn, amēn, I say unto you: I will perfect you in all fulness from the mysteries of the interior to the mysteries of the exterior and fill you with the spirit, so that ye shall be called 'spiritual, perfected in all fulness.'

And, amēn, amēn, I say unto you: I will give unto you all the mysteries of all the regions of my Father and of all the regions of the First Mystery, so that he whom ye shall admit on earth, shall be admitted into the Light of the height; and he whom ye shall expel on earth, shall be expelled from the kingdom of my Father in the heaven."

And so, Jesus continued, speaking of the third repentance of Pistis Sophia, where she cried out to the Light of powers to save her from the evil ones who sought to take away her light and power. "Let him in whom a sensitive spirit hath arisen, come forward and speak the thought of the repentance which Pistis Sophia hath uttered," Jesus declared.

And then, before Jesus had finished speaking, Martha came forward, fell down at his feet, kissed them, cried aloud and wept with lamentation and humbleness, saying: "My Lord, have mercy upon me and have compassion with me, and let me speak the solution of the repentance which Pistis Sophia hath uttered."

Jesus gave his hand unto Martha and said unto her: "Blessed is every one who humbleth himself, for on him they shall have mercy. Now, therefore, Martha, art thou blessed. But proclaim then the solution of the thought of the repentance of Pistis Sophia.

Mysteries and their meaning

It came to pass that, when John had finished speaking to Jesus about Pistis Sophia, Jesus continued to discourse with his disciples. He spoke of how Pistis Sophia was oppressed by the Self-willed emanations in the chaos and how she cried out in the fifth repentance. He said, "Light of my salvation, I sing praise unto thee in the region of the height and again in the chaos. I sing praise unto thee in my hymn with which I sang praise in the height and with which I sang praise unto thee when I was in the chaos."

Jesus then challenged his disciples to solve the thought of the fifth repentance of Pistis Sophia. And Philip, who was the scribe of all the discourses spoken by Jesus, stepped forward. However, Philip hesitated to tell the solution of the mysteries because he was only responsible for writing all the discourses and not speaking them.

Jesus then informed Philip, Thomas, and Matthew that they were enjoined by the First Mystery to write all the discourses and bear witness to the kingdom of heaven. He said, "Now, therefore, ye three have to write down all the discourses which I shall speak and [all things which I shall] do and which ye shall see, in order that ye may bear witness to all things of the kingdom of heaven."

Mary, who had been listening attentively, stepped forward and declared her readiness to hear and understand the word that Jesus had spoken. She spoke of the prophecy through Moses that stated, "By two or three witnesses shall every matter be established."

She believed that the three witnesses were Philip, Thomas, and Matthew, who were tasked with writing down all the discourses and bearing witness to the kingdom of heaven.

Jesus then said, "Who hath ears to hear, let him hear." And Mary, with her indweller of light, was ready to hear and discourse in openness with Jesus. She was eager to learn and understand the mysteries of the kingdom of the Light. And so, Jesus continued to discourse with his disciples, teaching them about the emanations, the chaos, Pistis Sophia, and the kingdom of the Light.

Jesus continued to speak to his disciples, saying, "It is written that when Pistis Sophia had completed her eighth repentance, she began to see the light of the Treasury more clearly. She saw that the First Mystery had indeed heard her cries for forgiveness and salvation and that her faith in the Light had not been in vain.

In her ninth repentance, she cried out to the Light, saying, "O Light, thou hast saved me from the chaos and oppression of the rulers of the twelve æons. Thou hast lifted me up from the darkness and brought me into a region which is not oppressed. I will sing thy praises and glorify thy name, for thou art my savior and my strength.

And in her tenth repentance, she declared, "Thou hast given me a new heart, O Light, and thou hast put within me a new spirit. Thou hast taken away my old heart of stone and hast given me a heart of flesh. Thou hast opened my eyes and made me see the truth. I will follow thee all the days of my life, for thou art my Lord and my God.

And so it was that Pistis Sophia was led out of the chaos and into the light of the Treasury. She was forgiven of her sins and was given a new life, a new spirit, and a new heart. And she praised the Light and gave thanks for its mercy and its salvation.

And Jesus concluded his discourse, saying, "This, my disciples, is the story of Pistis Sophia, who through her faith and repentance was saved from the chaos and brought into the light. And so it is with all who believe in the Light and trust in its mercy. For those who have faith will not be put to shame, but will be led out of the darkness and into the light."

And Jesus continued his discourse and said unto his disciples: "It was then when Pistis Sophia had spoken these words, that the time had come for her to be led out of the chaos. I, without the help of the First Mystery, sent forth a light power from within myself. This light power was sent down to the chaos with the mission of leading Pistis Sophia out of the deep regions of the chaos and up to the higher regions of the chaos, until the First Mystery would give the command to lead her entirely out of the chaos. My light power successfully led Pistis Sophia to the higher regions of the chaos.

However, when the emanations of Self-willed noticed that Pistis Sophia had been led out of the lower regions of the chaos and into the higher regions, they too followed after her, determined to bring her back into the lower regions. My light-power, which I had sent to lead Pistis Sophia out of the chaos, shone brightly. The emanations of Self-willed were in hot pursuit of Pistis Sophia as she was led into the higher regions of the chaos.

In response, Pistis Sophia sang praises and cried out to me, saying:

"I sing praises to thee, O Light. I longed to come to thee, and now thou hast saved me. I sing praises to thee, O Light, for thou art my deliverer. Leave me not in the chaos. Save me, O Light of the Height, for it is thou that I have praised. Thou hast sent me thy light through thyself and hast saved me. Thou hast led me to the higher regions of the chaos. May the emanations of Self-willed, who pursue me, sink down into the lower regions of the chaos, and let them not come to the higher regions to see me. May great darkness cover them, and a darker gloom come over them. Let them not see me in the light of thy power, which thou hast sent unto me to save me, so that they may not again get dominion over me."

"And let not their resolution, which they have formed to take away my power, take effect for them. And instead of taking my light from me, as they have spoken against me, let them have theirs taken instead. When Jesus had finished speaking these words unto his disciples, Salome came forward and said: "My Lord, thy power hath prophesied through Solomon, saying: 'I will give thanks unto thee, O Lord, for thou art my God. Abandon me not, O Lord, for thou art my hope. Thou hast given me thy vindication for naught, and I am saved through thee. Let them who pursue me, fall down and let them not see me. May a smoke-cloud cover their eyes and an air-mist darken them, and let them not see the day, so that they may not seize me. May their resolution be impotent, and may what they have devised come upon them. They have made a resolution and it hath not taken effect for them. They are defeated, although they be mighty, and what they have wickedly prepared has fallen upon them.'"

"And when Pistis Sophia had finished speaking these words in the chaos, I made the light-power, which I had sent to save her, into a light-wreath on her head. This way, the emanations of Self-willed would no longer have dominion over her. The light-wreath purified all the evil matters in Pistis Sophia and shook them, causing them to perish and remain in the chaos, while the emanations of Self-willed gazed upon them and rejoiced.

The First Mystery, which looketh without, continued speaking to John, the beloved brother. "The power which came out of the Height," the First Mystery said, "is I, sent by my Father to save Pistis Sophia from the chaos. I and the power that went from me, and the soul I received from Sabaōth, the Good, drew towards each other and became a single, shining light-stream."

The First Mystery then called upon Gabriēl and Michaēl, who were sent down into the chaos with the light-stream to help Pistis Sophia. When the light-stream shone in the chaos, the emanations of Self-willed were frightened, and the stream took the light-powers back from them, which they had taken from Pistis Sophia.

"Before I led Pistis Sophia out of the chaos," the First Mystery continued, "because it was not yet commanded by my Father, the First Mystery which looketh within, the emanations of Self-willed perceived that my light-stream had taken the light-powers back from them and poured them into Pistis Sophia. And when they saw Pistis Sophia again, they knew that she was stronger and more radiant than ever before."

The First Mystery then spoke of how Pistis Sophia was led out of the chaos, with the light-powers returned to her and the emanations of Self-willed powerless to stop it. "And this," the First Mystery declared, "is the truth which has sprouted forth from the earth, the power of Sabaōth, the Good, which entered the region of those of the Left and proclaimed the mysteries of the region of Truth."

"And you, John," the First Mystery continued, "are the righteousness which looked down from heaven, for you are the First Mystery which looketh down without. You came down from the spaces of the Height with the mysteries of the Light-kingdom and descended upon the light-vesture, which was Jesus, our Savior."

The First Mystery concluded by saying, "Well said, John, beloved brother. Your words have spoken the truth of the light-powers prophesied through David. May grace and truth continue to meet, and may righteousness and peace always kiss each other. May the power of Sabaōth, the Good, continue to shine forth and bring salvation to all."

The discourse of the First Mystery continued, as he spoke to his disciples about the teachings of Pistis Sophia. He explained how she had been saved from the chaos and darkness through the help of the light-stream. Pistis Sophia had cried out, saying that the light was all around her, saving her from the emanations of Self-willed and freeing her from the bonds of darkness.

Thomas then stepped forward and asked the First Mystery to give him guidance on the solution to the words that Pistis Sophia had spoken.

The First Mystery commanded Thomas to set forth the solution to the song that Pistis Sophia had sung to him. Thomas then proceeded to explain how the song of Pistis Sophia was related to the teachings of Solomon, the son of David, through his Odes.

According to Thomas, the words of Pistis Sophia, "I am saved from the bonds and am fled unto thee, O Lord," were echoed of the teachings of Solomon, who spoke of being saved by the Lord's right hand and being justified by his goodness. The words, "Thy power shone on my right and on my left and surrounded me on all sides of me, so that no part of me was without light," were also reflected in Pistis Sophia's words, "And thou hast covered me with the light of the stream."

Thomas further explained that the teachings of Solomon, "I was relieved of the coats of skin," were related to Pistis Sophia's words, "And they have purified me of all my evil matters, and I raised myself above them in thy light." The teachings of Solomon, "It is thy right hand which hath raised me up, and hath taken the sickness from me," were reflected in Pistis Sophia's words, "And it is thy light-stream which hath raised me up in thy light and hath taken from me the emanations of Self-willed which constrained me."

Finally, Thomas explained how the teachings of Solomon, "I have become powerful in thy truth and purified in thy righteousness," were related to Pistis Sophia's words, "I have become powerful in thy light and purified light in thy stream." The teachings of Solomon, "My adversaries have withdrawn themselves from me," were related to Pistis Sophia's words, "The emanations of Self-willed which constrained me, have withdrawn themselves from me."

The First Mystery praised Thomas for his understanding and wisdom, saying, "Well said, finely, Thomas, blessed one. This is the solution of the song which Pistis Sophia hath uttered." The First Mystery then continued to speak about Pistis Sophia and her continued praise and singing of songs unto him, as she thanked him for leading her down from the higher æon and up to the light.

Made in United States
Troutdale, OR
10/02/2023

13326414R00086